D0070339

NOT YET

Copyright © 2021 by Stanley Moss

All rights reserved. No part of this book may be reproduced, stored in a retrieval system, or transmitted in any form or by any means, including mechanical, electronic, photocopying, recording, or otherwise, without the prior written permission of the publisher.

SEVEN STORIES PRESS
140 Watts Street
New York, NY 10013
www.sevenstories.com

Distributed by PENGUIN RANDOM HOUSE

LIBRARY OF CONGRESS CATALOGING-IN-PUBLICATION DATA

Names: Moss, Stanley, author.
Title: Not Yet : Poems On China, Two Raw Fish Poems On Japan, American Poems Seasoned With Chinese Experience & New Poems, August 2020-May 2021
Description: New York : Seven Stories Press, [2021]
Identifiers: LCCN 2021020457 | ISBN 9781644211274 (paperback) | ISBN 9781644211281 (ebook)
Subjects: LCGFT: Poetry.
Classification: LCC PS3563.O885 N68 2021 | DDC 811/.54--dc23
LC record available at https://lccn.loc.gov/2021020457

Cover: Chinese Eye by Fu Xu

Printed in the U.S.A

NOT YET

Poems on China
Two Raw Fish Poems on Japan
American Poems Seasoned with Chinese Experience
& New Poems, August 2020 – May 2021

by

STANLEY MOSS

Seven Stories Press
New York • Oakland • London

Acknowledgements

The amazing and darling Michael Schmidt, publisher of sixteen-hundred books at Carcanet U.K, poet, novelist, literary historian, critic, teacher, suggested I publish a book of my Chinese poems. Thank you, Michael.
　　　　　–Stanley Moss

* * *

Most of the poems in *Poems on China, Two Raw Fish Poems on Japan*, and *American Poems Seasoned with Chinese Experience* have been published in various of Stanley Moss's books. Fifty-five poems from *Not Yet* are new, written between August 2020 and May 2021. They have been published in the *PN Review, Harvard Review, Shabdaguchha, The New Yorker, Literary Imagination, The Nation, The Guardian, Index on Censorship, The London Magazine* and *Best American Poetry 2020* and *2021*. Thirteen of these poems, translated into Chinese by Fu Hao, will appear soon in Chinese and English in *Poetry Periodical* of the China Writers Association.

Contents

Not Yet: Poems August 2020 – May 2021

* *

Dieu est le seul être qui, pour régner,
n'ait même pas besoin d'exister.
        —Charles Baudelaire

Whatever their personal faith,
all poets, as such,
are polytheists.
        —W.H. Auden

The wilderness and the solitary place shall be glad for them;
and the desert shall rejoice, and blossom as the rose.
        —Isaiah 35:1

A life in which the gods are not invited isn't worth living.
        —Roberto Calasso

Foreword

Stanley Moss With China in His Pen Hand
Willis Barnstone

Stanley and China are Mutt & Jeff, Gilbert & Sullivan, Superman & Dale Arden (the love interest of Flash Gordon), walking and racing through the sky, and Eve (the smart independent one) and Adam (the follower). Stanley loves to tune into the cosmos for a reference, a quotation, a proper name.

As an acrobat of fun, this tall verbal trickster transfers sand echoes of the Gobi Desert from Beijing streets into Moss song that he composes wherever he is and way up the Hudson River, where mythical periods far ago the Native Americans (originally Northern Chinese who wandered across the Bering Strait to fish and hunt in North and Latin American streams and jungles) wandered from multiple dynasties up to his railroad station in Riverdale (a fancy mainland in the Bronx). All these figures glow in his personal Sino Celestial Empire. He has scribbled them into infinity. From mythical Yellow Emperor, to poets Li Bai, Du Fu and Wang Wei, his renaissance brethren in the holy poetry racket.

His volume begins in China, then the U.S.A. with the birth of his Chinese godson Alexander Fu. Even Macedonian Alexander the Great (Αλέξανδρος ΓȺ ὁ Μακεδών) bows his mighty brow to the young American Chinese, whose birth portends a new portrait of the world. Alexander Fu gives up early intentions to be a cosmologist to become a composer of music. From China we drift to holy Japan, beautiful, political sexual three pages. Then there is a banquet of *American Poems Seasoned with Chinese Experience* only Stanley could cook up and finally eight months of Stanley Moss recent verse on any subject, from legendary Spanish Jews in Chinese Kaifeng to what he is cooking on his massive black steel stove.

Stanley chose me (I hope I don't disappoint) because for decades he has read me poem after poem, in draft after draft. I found them wondrous and told him so. I corrected a few things as editors do my junk, but the great river of verse continues. My left ear on Sundays, usually, became Moss ears. Meantime, Stanley published and edited my book *5 A.M. in Beijing*. Fun, always fresh and tart like grapefruit, poignant like exile, like death or residence on a star. A dog lover, from early Sancho honoring Don Quixote, Stanley's other, or any pet whom he treats with dignity. I know here is a little poem William Merwin loved:

NICKY

She danced into the moonless winter,
a black dog.
In the morning when I found her
I couldn't get her tongue back in her mouth.
She lies between a Japanese maple
and the cellar door, at no one's feet,
without a master.

Stanley Moss is never without an occasion. A frequent one is his birth or death. Here is a great self-minimizing poem that aims, uncovers a very wide scope from the Buddha to Provence in southern France. Through it all we overhear tones of his old friend Dylan Thomas, who also rode the world on a barrel of selected echoing words.

PRAYER

Give me a death like Buddha's. Let me fall
over from eating mushrooms Provençale,
a peasant wine pouring down my shirtfront,
my last request not a cry but a grunt.
Kicking my heels to heaven, may I succumb
tumbling into a rosebush after a love
half my age. Though I'm deposed, my tomb
shall not be empty; may my belly show above
my coffin like a distant hill, my mourners come
as if to pass an hour in the country,
to see the green, that old anarchy.

Stanley has always been fascinated by the beasts of this world. He transforms them into lovers, carries them to Canadian parks, to a swimming lake, to his house. They are equals or superiors, but he must care for them. To be a dog in the Moss house is a fine way to spend years on our globe.

ZOOPIE

I bought an abused dog in Canada,
a golden retriever.
I renamed him Zeus, I kissed him.
After a day he fell off the dock
to the bottom of Lake Corry.
I dived down twenty feet, brought him up by the collar.
Eventually he learned to swim. The day he first swam
he barked to come into the house
after chasing squirrels and deer in the woods.
I kissed Zoopie, for God's luck.

Stan is ever into world events. We have witnessed the rise and fall of a fake-blonde, would-be American dictator, who has managed to fabricate mini-Trumps, the proud, the corny, the armed, to terrorize our land with their multicolored racist coats. I heard many over the phone and then through the magic of email. But Stanley sees all in a political frame. He recalls, he associates, he expands, and brings in a whole period to furnish his venture. I would like to read aloud to you his amazing poem, *A Scream*.

Finally, Stan the Man is the unstoppable. That is his protection, his best, his tide of achievement. I like above all the fatal Ferryman, who waits for us all. I would like to quote the whole of *The Ferryman* here, but alas I will quote only the final lines.

I'm caught not saved, even though I praise
King David, Santa Teresa de Ávila
San Juan de la Cruz, the Ferryman who has
no name I know will eventually take me
by pole and his demon wings,
to an island where skeletons dance.

Now I think his accented Greek voice
is loud and clear. He's poling. He shouts my name,
I'm hiding. Clear across the Hudson Valley
I hear "Repent, repent." He's the double
of the statue of the murdered Commendatore
in Don Giovanni. I answer, "Your excellence,
Ferryman, statue, I invite you to dinner."
I've set the table with wine glasses,
New York State, Dutchess County red wine,
Hudson blue linen napkins,
knives, knives, knives, knives, no forks or spoons.
I know in a little while the Ferryman
will take me across the Styx in the company
of the four seasons, made human:
winter, spring, summer and autumn.
Summer wears a wreath of roses crowned with laurel,
Spring wears a waistcoat of budding dandelions,
Autumn, a coat of fallen maple leaves and grapevines,
wrinkled Winter has snowflakes in his hair and beard.
He wears ice snowshoes. I pretend to sleep.

The closing lines of *The Ferryman* proclaim him as a modern Hermes,
sending messages to the world. Our challenge. He invents language.
Now let us listen, be thoroughly infiltrated with the irreverent boy down
the block, with the challenger, with the Charlie Chaplin conscience of
our world, standing, if one can stand nicely on water, on an ocean of
uncertainty and brilliant wonder.

Preface

I hope you do not have to catch your breath,
watching me waltzing across a tightrope
as if there were no chance of my falling
into a pool of facts echoing facts.
I accuse myself of unseemly frivolity,
double focus and counterpoint.
Age 3, I lived near Liberty Avenue,
across the street from a Chinese laundry.
I noticed it was the first store to open.
the last to close at night, a river
of steam poured out of a glass door transom
Chinese writing on closed glass windows.
Someone told me if I put pink paper
under the laundry's door, it meant
someone died. They would close the store, run home.
I crossed the busy street alone, I did that.
They continued their fearless laundry work,
my criminal act, an angel of death memory.
My father believed in the Chinese proverb,
"Beat your son once every day, if you
 do not know a reason why, he does."
In winter, laundry steam melted snow and ice,
caressed cold skin under an overcoat.
In a summer heat wave, Chinese steam
blistered the screaming cement sidewalks.
Age 7, my teacher, Miss Murphy, told the class,
"You wouldn't want a Chinaman to move next door."
"Yes I would." She accused me of classroom treason,
"Go to the corner, face the wall for 10 minutes."

Lunar years later, some *Skull and Bone* heroes
wanted to kick me out of Yale Grad School
for supporting Mao, not Chiang Kai-shek,
who was advised by Nazi German generals.

13

Since I was seven, I painted poems,
as I do, about ancestors, nature, and gods.
The Chinese melted my heart of U.S. Steel
into a wildflower. I loved roses and briars,
daisies, dandelions, violets, the silk route.
In a lottery of butterflies I loved and won
the right to come out of my chrysalis.
I was knocked over by Waley's translations.
Pounds ideograms in *The Pisan Cantos*,
are my Saint Peter upside down mistakes,
when I worked for sinner and saint
taller than I was, James Laughlin the third.

I never, never loved a lady named Rose.
Lunar years passed. Barnstone got me invited
to teach English Lit in Beijing for a while.
I held Chinese friends close, then closer.
I breezed through Shinto, the Japanese mind,
beautiful temples, sacred and evil places.
I taught the King's English in Kyoto,
wrote on Japan two *Raw Fish Poems*.
Nanking, Guadalcanal, Hiroshima,
Fukushima, are not a daisy chain.
I was shaken by Japanese erotic art
that also had the purpose of selling
beautiful manufactured robes.

Next, *Poems Seasoned with Chinese Experience*,
distantly lighted by Chinese poetry.
I remember when President Kennedy was shot
Richard Wilbur broke down a church door
so he could pray at a Christian altar.
Look, the whole damned book
and last look is *Not Yet*.
It's November 2020 now;
still to come, perhaps nothing. I'll write

drop dead or last messages till April
2021. I will dance gravely.

Was it a floating log or a frog that taught me
if I tried to drown this book, it swims away?
Idle reader, I hope something in this book
will help you swim across a desert,
before I say "one, two, three – go, turn the page."
I might name this book *Impossibilities*.
I tell you, mongooses saw me swimming
across the Sahara, the Gobi, the Painted Desert,
the Negev, the Lemnos, impossible sands.
Off you go to Tudela, the Ebro valley,
meet the 12th century traveler Benjamin
of Tudela, celebrate the immaculate conception.
I would take it as a compliment if you say *Not Yet*
is a deadly sin that you fell asleep reading
and woke up, God in bed with you in the morning.

Poems on China

The Hawk, the Serpent, and the Cloud

In writing, he moved from the word *I*,
the word once a serpent curled between the rocks,
to *he*, the word once a hawk drifting above the reeds,
back to *we*: a nest of serpents.
Of course the hawk attacked the serpents.
She became a cloud, nursed us, mothered us,
scrubbed us with rain. *I*, once a serpent, know the Chinese
character for *he* is a standing figure,
the sign for *she* is a kneeling figure,
the word *cloud* is formed by two horizontal waves
above a plain, and that in writing Chinese
you must show feeling for different parts of the word.
Writing contains painting and painting writing.
Each is bird and sky to the other, soil and flower.

April, Beijing

Some of the self-containment of my old face
has been sandblasted away. The "yellow wind"
is blowing and my mouth and face burn
from the Gobi dust that scorches the city
after its historic passage over the Great Wall.
When I was young, I hosed the Atlantic salt
off my body—the salt was young too.

In China, "ashes to ashes and dust to dust"
means something more; work, no matter how cruel,
is part prophecy. Workers in the fields
that were Chinese eight thousand years ago,
their plows and terraces a kind of calligraphy,
face the living and the dead, whose windy fortress
takes on a mortal form: the Great Wall.
Even here the North Wind abducts a beauty.
Never before have I heard ancient laughter.
In China, I can taste the dust on my own grave
like salt. The winter coal dust shadows every wall
and window, darkens the lattice and the rose,
offers its gray society to the blue cornflower,
the saffron crocus, the red poppy.

The moon
brushed by calligraphy, poetry and clouds,
touched, lowered toward mortality—
to silk, to science, to paper,
requires that the word and painting respond
more intimately to each other, when the heart
is loneliest and in need of a mother,
when the ocean is drifting away,
when the mountains seem further off.

18

The birds sing in the dark before sunrise
because sunlight is delayed by dust and the sound
of a poet grinding his own ink from stone
according to the moon's teaching.
I am happy to be here, even if I can't breathe.
The emperor of time falls from a tree,
the dust rises.

Chinese Prayer

God of Walls and Ditches, every man's friend,
although you may be banqueting in heaven
on the peaches of immortality
that ripen once every three thousand years,
protect a child I love in China
and on her visits to the United States,
if your powers reach this far, this locality.
You will know her because she is nine years old,
already a beauty and an artist. She needs more
than the natural protection of a tree on a hot day.
You have so many papers,
more than the God of Examinations,
more than the God of Salaries,
who is not for me, because I am self-employed.
It may help you find her to know her mother
was once my bookkeeper,
her brother is a God in the family,
who at six still does not wipe his bottom.
Protect her from feeling worthless.
She is the most silent of children.
She has given me so many drawings and masks,
today I offered her fifty dollars for a painting.
Without a smile she answered,
"How much do you get for a metaphor?"
Sir, here is a little something to keep the incense burning,
remember her to the Almighty God whose character is Jade.

On Trying to Remember Two Chinese Poems

I've forgotten the book, the poet,
the beauty of calligraphy,
the poems made to be seen and read out loud,
two lost songs on hanging scrolls
stolen by foreigners . . .

White as frost,
a piece of freshly woven silk
made a fan, a bright moon.
She, or my lady, kept a fan nearby,
its motion a gentle summer breeze . . .
He dreaded the coming of autumn
when the north wind breaks the summer heat
and the fan is dropped unwanted
into a lacquer box,
its short term of favor ended.

A catalog of beds:
riverbed, flower bed, family bed.
My mother died when I was three,
dreadful to be a child in baby clothes.
I climbed into her bed and tried to nurse,
clutching her body with all my strength;
not knowing she was dead I spoke to her,
called to her. I remember thinking,
before, when I wept and ached for her,
although she was sick she came to me,
she whispered and caressed me,
then the lamp went out
and my mother coughed by the chilly window.
. . . A night of restless birds.

Without warning
a great forest fire, a devouring flame of wind,
rolling mountains of fire
with nothing to stop them but the sea.
Woman is half the sky.

Letter to an Unknown

Five centimeters, already Chinese,
in your mother's womb, pre-intellectual,
about sixty days. Sounds can see you,
music can see you. Fu Xu, your father,
I introduce you to him, he is a painter
already saving for your education, preparing
to carry you on his shoulders to museums.
Zhu Ming, your mother, holds you close
as it is possible to hold a being close,
rare as an Empress, Freudian Chinese therapist,
she will teach you the joys and sorrows
of writing Chinese. May you spend
many happy years washing ink from your hands.
You have made the Great Wall of China bleed.
Who am I? Something like a tree
outside your window: after you are born,
shade in summer, in winter my branches
heavy with snow will almost touch the ground,
may shelter deer, bear, and you.

Alexander Fu

Surrounded by a great Chinese wall of love,
he is already three weeks old and has a name.
His mother combs his hair with her hand, nurses him.
Soon he will learn the tragic news: the world is not all love.
He has already begun to earn a living,
a little of his poopoo was just put in a flower pot.
The least part of him bears the seal of his Manufacturer.

Alexander's First Battle

Now that you are looking over the edge of the world,
who will blame you for refusing to exchange
your mother's warm breast for rubber and warm glass?
Will you ever again be content? There will be laughter
and music, the solace of small talk, the solace
of art or science, twelve-year-old whiskey.
You will search the earth through hard years
to find somewhere in a timeless bed, or Venice,
or God forbid in the back seat of a car,
the return of such contentment. Alexander,
fight the bottle, fight it with all your being.
I will fight at your side.

Alexander Fu, Musing

The truth is I don't know the days of the week.
I can't tell time.
I have lived a summer,
a fall, a winter, an April, a May,
which I say because words are put in my mouth
because you-know-who is trying to sell something.
My mother rocks me to sleep, singing
a Chinese lullaby about crickets playing.
It's not easy to know so little,
but I wake to wonder, I touch wonder,
I play with wonder.
I smile at wonder.
I cry when wonder is taken from me.

Alexander Fu to Stanley

Big fool, my ancestors understood
we live in two societies: time and that other society
with its classes and orders, which you, Mr. America,
like to think you can ascend or descend at will.
Do I, a baby,
have to tell you there are laws that are not legislated,
judges neither appointed nor elected?
You are wetting your pants to talk to me.
Did it ever cross your mind I like to be ten months old,
going on eleven? You are trying to rob me of my infancy
because I have all the time in the world, and you don't.
On this May evening passing round the world
I probably have more diapers on the shelf
than you have years to go. I wish every time I shit
you'd have another year. Now that's an honest wish,
better than blowing out candles.
(Secretly you want to learn from me.)
You say I look like a prophet. Did it ever cross your mind
I would just like to be a bore like you?
Stop thinking about the Jew, Christian, Buddhist, Taoist thing!
The Long March wasn't from Kovno to Queens.
In summa: you are old and I am young,
that's the way it should be. I have better things to think about
than are dreamt of in your toilet-trained world.

Letter to Alexander Fu, Seven Years Old

A few days after your first birthday,
we had lunch on soup I made for grown-ups,
your father took you from your mother's arms,
carried you around our house to show you the sights;
he passed a painting of barren Sarah offering Hagar
to Abraham, old as I am. Then he stopped
before a half-naked lady looking in a mirror,
her two faces made you laugh.
In the library he showed you a family
resting on a hillside while their donkey grazed.
He did not tell you who they were, or that they were
on their way to Egypt.
He explained in Chinese and English:
"In this kind of painting, you must show the source of light.
The sunlight is behind the olive tree, the donkey
and sleeping father are in shade."
He named the colors, showed you a rainbow over a river.
You clapped hands and danced in his arms,
screeched so loud for joy, the dogs barked.
Next he came to an archangel with black wings
leading a boy carrying a fish.
He didn't tell you the boy will take fish gall,
put it into his father's eyes and cure his blindness.
Your father is a Chinese artist with a green card,
you are an American citizen in his arms.
Six years have passed. I read this letter to Alexander,
asked him what it meant.
He said, "It means Daddy likes me.
He should have explained in English before Chinese.
Abraham lived a hundred years,
had a baby and made God laugh.
God tells the heart what to do,
the heart tells the brain what to do.
I like that story, I want to take it home."

To Angelina, Whose Chinese Name Means Happiness

She lies naked, five days old,
a chance that history might be kindness and love,
a chance the size and strength of her hands—
the rarest Chinese-American beauty,
certain to break hearts.
May she teach her children Mandarin,
Tu Fu and calligraphy,
however busy the city.

May she know the joy of singing,
may she play a musical instrument,
may she find her own way in the wilderness.
Under the seven halts in the sky,
may she and her brother who is four
having sucked from the breast
of one mother, swear on her dark nipple
to be true to her nature.

I remember an ancient Chinese poet
saw a nine-year-old beauty
in a rose garden.
No one near the child
would speak except in whispers—
such was the power and burden of beauty.

After ten ancient years
the poet returned to marry her.
Later, the French and British
in Beijing ravished the sacred garden,
pillaged the Summer Palace.
It was not enough for the Brits
to have roses bloom at Westminster in December . . .
Angelina, you are five days old
and I have some 28,000 days.
If I were not married, I would wait.

To Alexander Fu on His Beginning and 13th Birthday

Severed from your mother, there was a first heartache,
a loneliness before your first peek
at the world, your mother's hand was a comb
for your proud hair, fresh from the womb—
born at night, you and moonlight tipped the scale
a 6lb 8oz miracle,
a sky-kicking son
born to Chinese obligation
but already American.
You were a human flower, a pink carnation.
You were not fed by sunlight and rain.
You sucked the wise milk of Han.

Your first stop, the Riverdale station,
a stuffed lion and meditation.
Out of PS 24, you will become
a full Alexander moon over the trees
before you're done. It would not please
your mother to have a moon god for a son.
She would prefer you had the grace
to be mortal, to make the world a better place.
There is a lesson in your grandmother's face:
do not forget the Way
of your ancestors. Make a wise
wish on your 13th birthday, seize the day
from history and geography.
If you lead, you will not lose the Way,
in your family's good company,
where wisdom is common as sunfish.
Protected from poisonous snakes by calligraphy:
paintings of many as the few, the few as many.
You already dine on a gluten-free dish
of some dead old King's English.

In your heart, keep Fu
before Alexander, and do
onto others as you would have others do
onto you.

To Alexander Who Wanted to Be a Cosmologist

September 27th and 28th,
two dark rainy days.
Alex was crying for no reason.
He said, "I thought summer was longer.
It's cold. It's already autumn."
Embraced, no one told him
you must learn to love
fall, winter, and spring.

I did not say beware of perfect happiness.
A tree without leaves is full of whispering.
Bats are 1/5th of the world's mammal
population. Viruses are polysexual.
Age 10, he wanted to be a cosmologist.
I write this 7 years later.
Alex looks down, fingering his computer.
He composes music, temperate melodies
made for all seasons.
I have his discarded fiddle
I will paint blue.

To Alexander Fu on His 18th Birthday

How distant the departure of you, a young boy.
The truth is not just a point of view.
It is a fact, and the truth today
is your birthday.
Was Tolstoy a good or bad boy?
He told the truth about war and peace.
I never heard him sing.
Today your birthday is worth a song.
A beautiful song is more beautiful
than a birthday cake. For good reasons,
your father taught you, in the twilight days of Tang,
Buddhist and Daoist literati gave life,
constructed a new art form
that joined poetry, music, and painting.
Poetry and calligraphy offered visualized thought.
Four tones used when speaking Chinese
give the same word different meanings,
gave the new works music and rhythm.
Your father smiled although in the past,
his laughter had been strangled.
A young man, you've just been given
a bedroom studio upstairs for your privacy and music.
Your computer music lyrics are mostly monosyllabic.
Computer music does not need a mouth,
needs fingering, electricity, or batteries.
I almost forgot your mother played Beethoven,
"Ode to Joy" from his 9th symphony,
on my 19th century Steinway piano;
she never had a piano lesson. A notorious
family thief wanted to be a singer.
Your music travels with the speed of light.
You may call your computer your dragon,
your compositions flute-free and gluten-free.
Still your music is Chinese-American

with a heart and soul, never Buddha-free.
Under your balcony, I've been fiddling with your music,
pun-intended. I think there is a chap
you prefer to kiss. May all the gods of China bless you
on your birthday. I do not wish you
many happy returns of the day,
because no day ever returns.
I wish you 365 happy days,
the impossible. Every place needs another
place. Darkness needs a lonely darkness
to make light. Verse needs silence and lonliness,
to make songs out of dumbfounded darkness,
because of the plague, reduced instrumentation.
Beyond desire, there is the mystery of the soul.
Be careful. Look to your right and left
when you cross the street.

            "Follow your heart!"
— advice given to me 70 years ago
by Djuna Barnes wearing a red and black cape,
waving her magic wand, a walking stick.
I was off to Spain for a better life and death.
It does not always work, but it embraces the truth:
a good companion, in or out of bed,
close to hell and on Easy Street.

Thanksgiving 2020

At a distance I write
           in my notebook
where Siamese elephants dance
           tusk to tusk.
I write a play within a play
           a tragic farce,
curtain going up forever.
At the Thanksgiving table naked I sit drinking
           and writing what I must,
because I love the Fu family.
           Mother and son believe, hold dearly
President Obama was born in Africa,
           Americans read fake news
in *The New York Times* and *Washington Post,*
           climate change caused by us, a hoax.
The facts, a nightmare: Alexander
           voted to export Dreamers
he voted to export himself.
           He needed to be "spoken to"
as they used to say.
           He is an exceptional welcome dreamer
according to his mom
who always speaks to me ex cathedra.

Sitting on a prehistoric rock
           I talk and sing
outside the Peking opera house
           in Tiananmen square.
I'm not proud I tried to make a rocking chair
           out of Stone Age rock.
An invisible menace
           methane flares
      are scorching birds
in United States landfills.

A while ago, Zhou Enlai was asked
do you consider the French Revolution
              a success?
He answered "It's too early to tell."
I consider all stories love stories.
Was the story I just told true, a success?
              Did I reach the end of the story?
It's too early to tell.

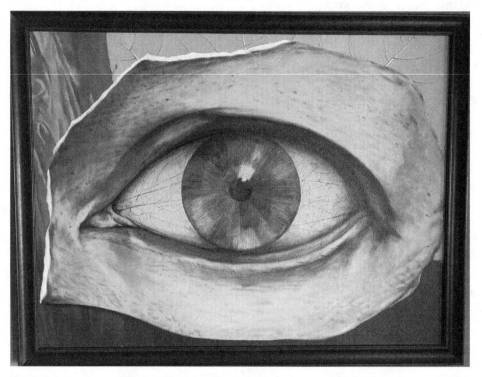

Chinese Eye by Fu Xu, 2018

Year of the Rooster

Good days are eggs, time a mother hen.
This year is the Chinese Year of the Rooster.
Another moon year gone, this rooster brings
"Good luck! Honesty! Fidelity!"
He wakes the world from sleep
that sees everything with closed eyes,
because everything that lives
has sweet dreams and nightmares.
There are Xia to Ming,
Spider and Scorpion Tales not for children—
except the tale The Happy Spider,
who would not eat meaty flies—
he lived on grapes and wine,
flying rice, got drunk.
The Emperor Rooster,
father of good days, chick dynasties,
has suffered year after year
watching his hens in the yard
running around with their heads cut off.
This morning, he simply doesn't appear,
in his yard or timeless hen houses.
News in the marketplace and Tiananmen Square:
the Emperor Rooster is in China,
China is celebrating him,
the 4,715th year
since, cock of the walk, he came into the world.

De que mal morira?

Year of the Monkey

Goya etched a donkey that sat
for a monkey painting his portrait,
a donkey aristocrat.
To show you where I'm at when I first saw that
on a smartphone, the sunlight
outside the Mid-Hudson Credit Bank,
hurt my eyes. It was so bright
I saw the donkey painting a monkey.
Hóu, monkey in Chinese,
is a sign of the zodiac.
I celebrate the year of the monkey.
We play with them, they play with us.
Mother and child play Mary and Jesus
in a zoo. In beginning light monkeys were created
before the garden where Adam and Eve mated.

Time passes, some castration, not much circumcision,
except in Fuzhou that keeps Jewish tradition.
Every monkey, day, and night is precious,
Goya's monkey and donkey are capricious.
Goya did not paint himself dead.
He paints himself before he dies. He etched
a bad death, a donkey eating a sleeping man,
then he died from eating white paint lead.
Art looks for truth, photography lies.
A year is an invention, something human,
the year of the monkey is something more human.
Ancestors, sky and earth are sacred.
Buddha deniers practice dirty trade, murder, hatred.

In Zigong, Salt City of China

In Zigong, salt city of China,
the spring rain suddenly stopped.
On the first summer day sunlight went deep
into the ravines. In the cold climate,
I chose to walk in an unfamiliar garden.
There were peach blossoms to the west
and plum blossoms toward the east wall.
Although I walked alone, I said "Beauty, beauty."
I did not say peach blossoms were not as white
as plum blossoms. The peach blossoms fell into a rage,
flaming red to the very roots of their hair,
their faces redder and redder with accusation.
But I intended no harm, no offense.
There was no reason for anger.
Pity me on my birthday, the first day of summer,
when the flowers have their ways completely beyond me.

Moss at the Forbidden City, 1986

38

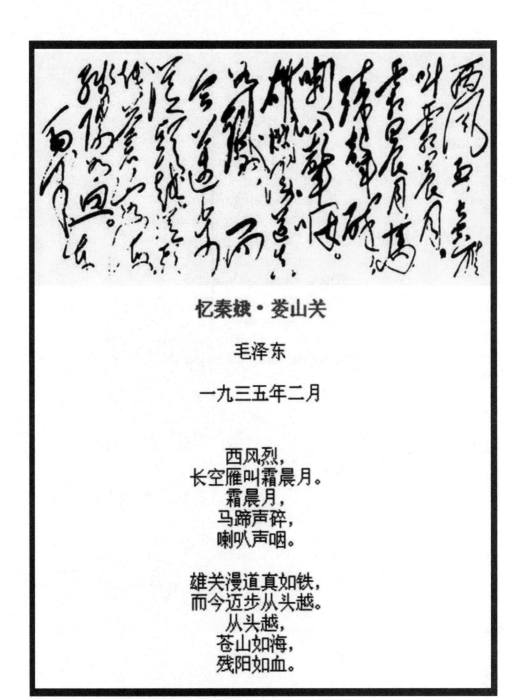

忆秦娥·娄山关

毛泽东

一九三五年二月

西风烈，
长空雁叫霜晨月。
霜晨月，
马蹄声碎，
喇叭声咽。

雄关漫道真如铁，
而今迈步从头越。
从头越，
苍山如海，
残阳如血。

Loushan Pass by Mao Zedong

LOUSHAN PASS

A hard West Wind,
In the vast frozen air wild geese shriek to the morning moon.
Frozen morning moon.
Horse hoofs shatter the air
And the bugle sobs.

The grim pass is like iron
Yet today we will cross the summit in one step,
Cross the summit.
Before us greenblue mountains are like the sea,
The dying sun like blood.

Translation by WILLIS BARNSTONE

Murder
written 2020

The great poet murderer Chairman Mao
wrote nothing like a revolutionary sonnet
in calligraphy. Forever, then, and now
even if you can't read it, his poetry is beautiful
After the Long March the great famine came,
people ate rats, blood was champagne.
Mao Zedong was milk, the one tit
that allowed the infant China to exist.
Mao's first wife was mentally ill, he said,
"I'll make her a sane, happy communist."
He sent her to Moscow for ten red,
red years, Mao's favorite color, not the green
green that Lorca loved. He let temples
stand, but he cut off the heads of Buddhas.
Mao could write a poem beautifully simple,
a gift with a Little Red Book to the people,
the same day murder a village of do-gooders.
I paint good news on a krater, neither fake:
The word poetry comes from the Greek, to make,
the Chinese character is to keep.
A rattlesnake, I want to make and keep.

                    * * *

I thought of murdering a lady
who was destroying my son, the reason
I sent her roses wrapped in poison ivy.
April. T.S. Eliot dedicated *The Waste Land*
to il miglior fabbro Ezra Pound.
With breeding lilacs in hand
Pound cheered, raved for Mussolini.
He wished all the Jews were given gas
in death camps. There were great poet meanies,
Neruda was a kind Stalinist, alas.
There was one Jorge Luis Borges,

one Paul Celan, one Seamus Heaney.
The ship of life is sinking, poetry is a lifeboat,
wintery death murders, poets give us an overcoat.
Roethke was a racist. I don't see Theodore
waltzing at lynchings. (I see anti-Semites galore,
from the empire state's cellar to the top floor.)
Will Burroughs, writer, "gunshot painter," shot
his wife dead, both of them on H and pot.
I believe in the very right and very wrong,
not sin. Nothing is worse than murdering,
I've heard someone murdering a song.
There's still an electric chair at Sing Sing,
I had a distant cousin who sat in it,
a poet did not throw the switch.
Anyway, the Lord was mistaken to think
"I'll murder" is the same as doing it.
I'm going uphill, I'll never reach the summit.
I sew a poem together stitch by stitch.
Camels pass through the eye of a needle,
the devil plays hymns on a fiddle.
The days of our years are threescore and ten,
rich men get more years than poor men.

* * *

I cannot forget great poet and murderer Mao
not soon or after, now,
a disguised American I will sip his cup of tea.
I will stir every line with the spoon, "kill."
Kill. I is a dangerous word. Never forget
Kill. the pronoun <u>we</u> confiscates private property.
Kill. Alone, Mao's ideas are not private property.
Kill. Dine with two people, three can't keep a secret.
Kill. One child take care. If you beget
Kill. a girl, should you want to keep her, you have a debt.
Kill. You owe a son to the people's army.
Kill. A puppy sandwich tastes better than salami.
Kill. Peasants and factory workers know by heart

Kill. the poetry of Tu Fu.
Kill. Buddhist death is a work of art.
Kill. I still want poetry that "makes it new."
Kill. Suffering and grief are teachers.
Kill. if life were cinema, life's one reel
Kill. life is not a double feature.
Kill. Be civil, run away from evil,
Kill. beware of the white peril.

China Poem

In China, the people give importance
to what they call "spring couplets," paper sayings
pasted with wheat-flour and water
above and down the sides of doorways
ancient and just built.
On the entrance to a cave house,
I saw, right side, on red paper, in calligraphy:
"Strive to Build Socialist Spiritual Civilization."
On the left, on pink paper:
"Intellectuals: Cleaning Shithouses for Ten Years
in the Cultural Revolution Clears the Head."
Across the lintel:
"When Spring Comes Back, the Earth is Green."
The Chinese know they enter and depart
through the doors of poetry. I was on my way
to the Great Wall that can be seen from outer space.
Wondering, I stopped at a rural place.
Stranger, I was greeted lovingly
by an old mother. I was offered tea,
welcomed into her one room stone house.
There was a framed photograph
of a young man on a table, some books,
a red brick stove bed for a family.
I told He Huaren, a dead poet's wife,
"In that room, I saw a great civilization."
On our way, we passed a cemetery.
Two women and a man
kneeled at the grave of a dead ancestor,
touched their heads to the ground.
Then, standing up, they burned paper money.
From the distance, I saw fireworks lighting
half the sky in the afternoon thirty years ago.

Two Raw Fish Poems on Japan

The Poem of the Pillow

I believe love saves the world from heartbreak.
I'm learning to play the concrete harp.
I'm tired of traveling by my name only.
It is time for tears held back and washed away,
days that mean "yes" and nights that mean "no."
Look, the moon never disconsonant,
lies down, sleeps under a bridge.
Still, when I am asleep, at breakfast,
reading a book or walking across a street
thinking I am far from eternal sloth, a God
for his comfort will push me out of sight.

Veiled Fortuna, because knowing who you were,
I made you laugh and gave you pleasure
when you opened your mortal dressing gown.
Fortuna, I dare not say what I'm thinking,
please, please
give me proof that has no text—life everlasting
is to be loved at the moment of death.
Now my thoughts drift to a Japanese woodcut:
a sacred lake, a child's sailboat, the shore
a woman's open thighs, her gorgeous vulva.
At a distance, a flowering plum mouths a tall pine.
Deep within her leaves there is a poem of the pillow.

47

The Decadent Poets of Kyoto

Their poetry is remembered for a detailed calligraphy
hard to decipher, less factual than fireflies in the night:
the picture-letters, the characters, the stuff
their words were made from were part of the meaning.
A word like "summer" included a branch of plum blossoms,
writing about "summer in a city street"
carried the weight of the blossoming branch,
while "a walk on a summer afternoon"
carried the same beautiful purple shade.

They dealt with such matters distractedly,
as though "as though" were enough, as though
the little Japanese woman with the broom
returning to her husband's grave to keep it tidy
was less loving than the handsome woman in the café
off the lobby of the Imperial Hotel,
who kissed the inside of her lover's wrist.
In their flower arrangements, especially distinct
were the lord flower and emissary roses—

public representations now shadows.
Their generals and admirals took musicians
with them to war, certain their codes
would not be deciphered, in an age when hats
and rings were signs of authority and style.
They thought their secrets were impenetrable,
they thought they had the power to speak and write
and not be understood, they could hide the facts
behind a gold-leaf screen of weather reports.

It was Buddha who had an ear for facts:
coins dropping into the ancient cedar box,
hands clapping, the sound of temple bells and drums.
Codes were broken, ships sank, men screamed
under the giant waves, and a small hat
remained afloat longer than a battleship.

American Poems Seasoned with Chinese Experience

For Margaret

My mother near her death
is white as a downy feather.
I used to think her death was distant
as a tropical bird, a giant macaw, whatever that is—
a thing I have as little to do with
as the Chinese poor.
I find a single feather of her suffering
I blow it gently as she blew
into my neck and ear.

A single downy feather is on the scales,
opposed by things of weight, not spirit.
I remember the smell of burning feathers.
I wish we could sit upon the grass
and talk about grandchildren
and great-grandchildren.
A worm directs us into the ground.
We look alike.

I sing a lullaby to her about her children
who are safe and their children.
I place a Venetian lace tablecloth
of the whitest linen on the grass.
The wind comes with its song
about things given that are taken away
and give again in another form.

Why are the poor cawing, hooting,
screaming in the woods?
I wish death were a whip-poor-will
the first bird I could name.
Why is everything so heavy?
I did not think

she was still helping me to carry
the weight of my life.
Now the world's poor are before me.
How can I lift them one by one in my arms?

The Lost Brother

I knew that tree was my lost brother
when I heard he was cut down
at four thousand eight hundred sixty-two years;
I knew we had the same mother.
His death pained me. I made up a story.
I realized, when I saw his photograph,
he was an evergreen, a bristlecone like me
who had lived from an early age
with a certain amount of dieback,
at impossible locations, at elevations
over 10,000 feet in extreme weather,
on Savage Mountain his company: other conifers,
the rosy finch, the rock wren, the raven and,
blue and silver insects that fed mostly off each other.
Some years bighorn sheep visited in summer—
he was entertained by red bats, black-tailed jackrabbits,
horned lizards, the creatures old and young he sheltered.
Beside him in the shade, pink mountain pennyroyal—
to his south, white angelica.
I am prepared to live as long as he did
(it would please our mother),
live with clouds and those I love
suffering with Buddha.
Sooner or later, some bag of wind will cut me down.

Nicky

She danced into the moonless winter,
a black dog.
In the morning when I found her
I couldn't get her tongue back in her mouth.
She lies between a Japanese maple
and the cellar door, at no one's feet,
without a master.

The Bathers

1.

In the great bronze tub of summer,
with the lions' heads cast on each side,
couples come and bathe together: each touches only
his or her lover, as he or she falls back
into the warm eucalyptus-scented waters.
It is a hot summer evening and the last
sunlight clings to the lighter and darker blues
of grapes and to the white and rose plate
on the bare marble table. Now the lovers
plunge, surface, drift—an intruding elder
would not know if there were six or two,
or be aware of the entering and withdrawing.
There is a sudden stillness of water,
the bathers whisper in the classical manner,
intimate distant things. They are forgetful
that the darkness called night is always present,
sunlight is the guest. It is the moment
of departure. They dress, by mistake exchange
some of their clothing, and linger
in the glaring night traffic of the old city.

2.

I hosed down the tub after five hundred years
of lovemaking, and my few summers.
I did not know the touch of naked bodies
would give to bronze a fragile gold patina,
or that women in love jump in their lovers' tubs.
God of tubs, take pity on solitary bathers
who scrub their flesh with rough stone
and have nothing to show for bathing
but cleanliness and disillusion.

Some believe the Gods come as swans,
showers of gold, themselves, or not at all.
I think they come as bathers: lovers
whales fountaining, hippopotami
squatting in the mud.

Song of Imperfection

Whom can I tell? Who cares?
I see the shell of a snail protected by a flaw
in its design: white is time, blue-green is rot,
something emerging in the rough dust, the unused
part of a shape that is furious and calm.
In aging grasses, knotted with their being,
the snail draws near the east bank of the pond,
not because that is where the morning sun is,
but out of coastal preference, raising
a tawny knotted counterwhirl
like a lion cub against its mother's haunch,
anus of a star. But let the conch stand
in the warm mud, with its horn become an eye,
suffering the passion of any snail:
a hopeful birth, a death, an empty tomb.
I'd walk with this horned eye, limp-foot after limp-foot,
beyond the dry wall of my life, backward
into the sacramental mud, where the soul begins to reason—
as on that afternoon Aristotle dissecting
squid proclaimed "the eternity of the world."
There is not a thing on earth without a star
that beats upon it and tells it to grow.

When I Played a Buddhist Priest, Etc.

1

I lived in flight from an apartment,
desolate as Beethoven's jaw. On the go
actor, I could put my life aside,
I drank till my feet turned purple
or into goat hooves. I could play the serpent,
Eve, Adam, the apple before or after it was bit.
I wandered beside myself, a figure far from myself
as orange rind: I could turn from David into Saul weeping—
to Absalom, his hair caught in a tree. I could play my own fool,
my own column of cloud, the presence of God.
I could throw myself out into the garbage,
or, like a child's top on a string,
turn red and blue then whirl into a single color.
I played a Buddhist priest reading from his Book
into the ear of a corpse who hears
the reader's voice telling him all his visions
are his own unrealized, undiscovered forms,
the horrible furies and the calm
he must come to understand are his.

2

"Far below the salt cliffs," I wrote in my Hymn Book,
"the river's violin has emptied into the sea."
Only the man-bird flies from the Dead Sea to the Himalayas,
from the ancient dead shrouded in poetry
to the never-ending ice so thick,
the dead are ritually butchered and fed to vultures
that, surrounded by haloes of the sun,
rise like doves out of the jeweled snow.
In the glacial silence a man's leg-bone
makes a sweeter whistle than your ram's horn.

3

To bathe at birth, marriage and death, a rule in Tibet,
was not enough even for me. "No one has ever slid down
the Himalayas so fast," I said in a coarse aside.
Unteachable, I learned, I fell
more like Richard the Second than Adam.
In a farce I came closest to the stinking breath
of my own mortality, trying to lift
a snapping turtle off Deerfield road,
it bit into my shoe, I fell back into a crabgrass ditch—
broke my ankle and elbow.
It was Memorial Day, a day
I broke my veteran's bones on three occasions.

4

What do I know that no one knows?
The care I wanted to give, that no one else would give.
I had lived to sing to my dying mother
beside her bed. Now memory's my mother, she keeps
my life from burning off like morning mist.
One black tear at the corner of my left eye,
I wept over a glass of spilled milk. I pretended
to play Mozart on a violin without lessons.
I bought myself a fiddle and a bow
strung with circus-horse hair,
an earthly bow, not a rainbow.
Who was I to know so many tunes?
I just played my everyday music—
I would never wrap the holy name letters
around my fingers. I wrote a song that began:
"I fall back from making love to the kind of day it is. . . ."
I cannot escape the jail of poetry,
books books books books not stone.
Love came into my cell,
she is jailed with me. A lady's absence
keeps her in my prison without a word.

Hermaphrodites in the Garden

1.

After the lesson of the serpent there is the lesson
of the slug and the snail—hermaphrodites,
they prosper on or under leaves, green or dead,
perhaps within the flower. See how slowly
on a windless day the clouds move over the garden
while the slug and the snail, little by little pursue
their kind. Each pair with four sexes
knows to whom it belongs, as a horse knows
where each of its four feet is on a narrow path:
two straight below the eyes, two a length behind.
There is cause and reason for,
but in the garden, mostly life befalls.
Each male female lies with a male female,
folds and unfolds, enters and withdraws.
On some seventh day after a seventh day they rest,
too plural for narratives, or dreams, or parables,
after their season. One by one they simply die—
in no special order each sex leaves the other
without comfort or desire.

2.

I open my hands of shadow and shell that covered my face—
they offered little protection from shame or the world.
I return to the garden, time's mash of flowers,
stigmas and anthers in sunlight and fragrant rain.
Human, singular the slug of my tongue
moves from crevice to crevice, while my ear,
distant cousin of a snail, follows the breathing
and pink trillium of a woman who is beautiful
as the garden is beautiful beyond joy and sorrow,
where every part of every flower is joy and sorrow.
I, lost in beauty, cannot tell which is which,
the body's fragrant symmetry from its rhymes.
I am surrounded by your moist providence.
A red and purple sunrise blinds me.

The Swimmer

I remember her first as a swimmer:
I saw my mother swimming in a green and white bathing suit,
her arms reaching out across giant ocean waves,
swimming through the Atlantic breakers.
I stood on the shore,
knowing almost nothing, unable to go to her—
dumbfounded by the wonder of it,
It happened long before I could dress myself.
I was a little older than the weeping Chinese child
sitting alone in the rubble of Nanking—
barely old enough to be read to,
not able to tell time or count.
When I had that kind of knowledge, in her old age
she showed me herself naked, the tubes and the sack.
An hour later she said, "I must have been crazy."
Then she swam off again and never came back.
For a few days I awoke as that child again.
Now I have learned a kind of independence.
It is mostly in dreams she comes back, younger or older,
sometimes fresh from the joy of the swim.

Moss near Naples, 1948

Spoon

to Jane Freilicher

I was scribbling, "Goya painted with a spoon" when I heard Jane died,
I knew enough not to be surprised but I was.
Saturn gnawed his son without a place setting.
I never got over the Berliner Ensemble's Mother Courage,
when she screamed, "I bargained too much"
(for her murdered son's life).
The actress wore a wooden spoon as a brooch.
Tongue tied, I kept "spoon." It is not a decoration.

In a daydream, I avow without reason
Jane Freilicher painted with a spoon—
potato fields, Watermill, pink mallow,
her early painting Leda and the Swan,
nothing we see—and with everyday palette knife,
brushes or late-invented forks,
useful for painting hydrangeas and eyelashes,
proof painters work like translators,
English into Chinese, everyday English words:
daylight, flower, woman, moon
are different in Ming, Tang, and Song:
different characters, different calligraphy.

She painted with a silver or oak spoon
ponds or stars, bones were oblong and triangles,
nothing we see. She painted light, mastered it, was mastered by it,
moved the world by "tipping the horizon up."
My honor: from a distance she painted
my house on Mecox Bay, my Corinthian columns,
my garden and sandpit
along the old Montauk road, my beach plums,
fireweed, roses of Sharon, day lilies, love
mostly washed out by hurricanes.

I say "my" but I never thought
I had good title to anything or anyone.
Then there was her battle of dreams
versus hallucinations, battles without a heroine,
the color of fate, breathtaking, inevitable colors.
She would never forgive
those who think painting and poetry
function about the same as wallpaper.
Sometimes she painted small pictures
easily hidden from search parties
as Goya did, hiding from the Inquisition
because he painted nudes,
Protestant fields, Catholic fields, Jewish fields, like her.
She suffered the heresies of the Hamptons
where most painters of roses, whatever their personal faith,
and all poets, as such, are polytheists.
Again, she studied the many moods
of the sun and ocean through a window.
I studied Chinese at the Beijing railroad station,
eight thousand years or so of Chinese faces.
Every Chinese knows five cardinal relations:
ruler subject, father son, husband wife,
elder and younger brother, friend and friend.
I share the undiscovered country that begins
at the Southampton railroad station,
the beauty and color of Long Island
in the mist . . .
I sit shivering with the old-timers, gossiping
about the steam engines
from Penn Station to Montauk
100 years ago, faster than now, the island's
chestnut trees harvested for firewood,
the cemeteries, a little away from the railroad tracks,
cornflowers and poppies,
off Routes 114, 27, Springs Fireplace Road,

overloaded with painters,
I kiss my Yoricks. I knew them well.

*

Jane, we watched the pagan ocean
that holds bottom feeders
that thrive in fiery volcanic waters,
and birds that never come ashore.
Often we met at the beach, half-naked,
barefooted or in sandals.
We knew where fifty-six swans nested,
that Long Island painters seldom painted
the night, or character. We chased whales,
saved wounded seals.
After an Atlantic hurricane, in our trees
with salt-drenched curled leaves,
thousands of fooled monarch butterflies gathered
on their way to Mexico.
We embraced 65 years ago—
not a long time for a redwood,
a long time for an oak or an elm.

The day you died,
I wish ex cathedra, Pope Francis said, "dogs go to heaven,"
so fawns, foxes, and rabbits aren't left behind.
You understood shadow.
At first look, you never painted sorrow.
You picked up stemless flowers, homeless
like beauties standing on street corners,
gorgeous juvenile delinquents.

The Debt

1.

I owe a debt to the night,
I must pay it back, darkness for darkness
plus interest.
I must make something out of almost nothing,
I can't pay back by just not sleeping
night after night. I hear them screaming
in the streets of New York, "What? What? What?"

I can't write a check to the night,
or a promissory note: "I'll write songs."
Only the nightmare is legal tender.
I bribe owls, I appeal
to the creatures of the night: "Help me
raccoons, catfish, snakes!"
I put my head in the tunnel of a raccoon,
pick up a fish spine in my mouth.
Perhaps the night will accept this?
Dying is my only asset.

These days driving along I turn up my brights.
I love and am grateful for anything that lights
the darkness: matches, fireworks, fireflies.
My friend who's been to Tibet in winter
tells me when the sun is high against the ice
you see the shadow of the earth.
The night after all is just a shadow . . .
The debt keeps mounting.
I try to repay something by remembering
my Dante, the old five and ten thousand lira notes
had Dante's face etched on the front.
(I bought that cheap.) Hard cash to the night
is finding out what I do not want to know
about myself, no facts acceptable,

a passage through darkness,
where the one I stop to ask, "Why? What?"
is always myself I cannot recognize.

2.
If only I could coin nightmares:
a barnyard in Asia,
the last dog and cat betrayed, are no more.
A small herd of three-legged blind cows
still gives milk.
A pig with a missing snout, its face like a moon,
wades in a brook.
A horse, its mane burnt to cinders,
a rear hip socket shot off, tries to get up,
thrusting its muzzle into the dark grass.
A rooster pecks without a beak or a coxcomb.
A rabbit that eats stones, sips without a tongue,
runs without feet.
A ditch of goats, sheep and oxen
locked in some kind of embrace.
All move their faces away,
refuse the charity of man
the warrior, the domesticator.
I see a whale with eyes yards apart
swimming out of the horizon,
surfacing as if it were going to die,
with a last disassociated vision,
one eye at peace
peers down into the valley and mountains
of the ocean, the other eye floats,
tries to talk with its lids to the multitude.
While in the great head
what is happening and what happened mingle,
for neither has to be.
I pray for some of my eyes to open and some to close.
It is the night itself that provides
a forgiveness.

In the Swim

1

I'm in the swim. I won't swim across the River Styx
that is out of fashion, like the Phoenix
that lived 500 years. I am not merry
swimming to any kind of cemetery
dictionary.
I'd rather swim the Charles to a library
drink Bloody Marys with Christopher Ricks.
Toward an island of dancing skeletons,
I pole my boat, my passengers the seasons,
paradise offers eternal life without seasons.
It's silly to think rivers belong to anyone.
It's time to write about rivers I've known,
not underground, but rivers legible to mosquitos,
black flies, a beaver, the human eye—
poisoned, damned up. A stone's throw
from their own riverbeds, they cry
out in pain, flood, are never foolish, groan,
know laughter, have children called brooks,
who, afraid, run to them, scribble on stone.
You who read and write books
with bays, waterfalls, tidal sentences, look
at a river that is a person,
who tells old wives' tales about the ocean.

In the name of no Father and no Son,
I will never swim across the Mekong
or join Yeats bringing the Liffey swans
promised by his friend Oliver
when he swam across the river—
the Black and Tans'
bullets breaking water near his head like salmon.
(Gogarty loved a party, his bawdy poetry at Trinity
made him a favorite among the dons.)

2

Zeus, an eagle, flew over the Meander,
held Ganymede, a beauty, in His claws—
lightning and hail—a pause,
then thunder.
Some waters are feeders, some devour
wilderness in an hour.
The Ganges shows eternal mercy,
the dead set afire with floating flowers,
the River Jordan is salty, full of heresy—
bathe in it, get in the swim, with scribbled stone
glacial ideas broken
off from upriver mountains
scrawled on rock "Give to the poor everything you own."

I never tried to wash off my sins
I wanted to keep. Heaven is a small town.
God keeps His word
to rivers, that are oratorios without words,
half notes, quarter notes, clefs are fish and birds.
Whenever, wherever His day begins,
God's day is not our day.
We are musical scores, we hear ourselves
say hello hello, farewell farewell.

May the last song I sing bring
joy and remembrance to others.
Rivers trust in the Beginning,
leave empty beds, their sisters and brothers.
Over the Yangtze there are bridge-temples,
sure as Buddha had big ears and dimples.
Bridges separated good life from bad death,
bad life from good death.
I sit near a bridge and watch the trees grow.
In China, the past is wherever you go.
I dive to find the great beneath.

I will not rhyme, I'll swim freestyle to my death.
Come swim with me, idle readers,
spend a while under water. I notice
rivers flow to blue harbors under the ice,
cubist sunlight indifferent to changing seasons.
I see the curtain fall, actors in underwater theaters,
players in make-up, the cast: Buddha, Jehovah, Christ.
You there, look for me in holy places, I shout
"praise the Lord," among pickerelweeds and bottom feeders,
I'm clothed in spawn of many fish, on shore it's rutting season.
I hold on to uncertainty, mystery, doubt
without any irritable reaching out
after fact and reason.

Sleep

These days I doze off, sleep longer.
Sleep drags me off, first by inches,
then by yards—
now miles closer to eternity
that is another name for poverty.
So sleep steals my wallet.
It should be shackled, jailed,
allowed a period of recreation,
time off for good behavior,
paroled. As for me, I have life to live,
work to do, books to read.
Think of me as one of those
old rice wines.
Let me get dusty, decant me
after one hundred years;
do not put me on ice.
Drink me in the garden
on a summer evening. Get drunk.

The Meeting

It took me some seconds as I drove toward
the white pillowcase, or was it a towel
blowing across the road, to see what it was.
In Long Island near sanctuaries
where there are still geese and swans,
I thought a swan was hit by an automobile.
I was afraid to hurt it. The beautiful creature
rolled in sensual agony,
then reached out to attack me.
Why do I feel something happened on the road,
a transfiguration, a transgression,
as if I hadn't come to see what it was,
but confronted the white body,
tried to lift it, help her fly
or slit its throat.
Why did I need this illusion
a beauty lying helpless?

Squall

I have not used my darkness well,
nor the Baroque arm that hangs from my shoulder,
nor the Baroque arm of my chair.
The rain moves out in a dark schedule.
Let the wind marry. I know the Creation
continues through love. The rain's a wife.
I cannot sleep or lie awake. Looking
at the dead I turn back, fling
my hat into their grandstands for relief.
How goes a life? Something like the ocean
building dead coral.

Listening to Water

Water wanted to live.
It went to the sun,
came back laughing.
Water wanted to live.
It went to a tree
struck by lightning.
It came back laughing.
It went to blood. It went to womb.
It washed the face of every living thing.
A touch of it came to death, a mold.
A touch of it was sexual, brought life to death.
It was Jubal, inventor of music,
the flute and the lyre.
"Listen to waters," my teacher said,
"then play the slow movement
of Schubert's late *Sonata in A*,
it must sound like the first bird
that sang in the world."

Clams

Ancient of Days, bless the innocent
who can do nothing but cling,
open or close their stone mouths.
Out of water they live on themselves
and what little seawater they carry with them.
Bless all things unaware that perceive
life and death as comfort or discomfort:
bless their great dumbness.

We die misinformed
with our mouths of shell open.
At the last moment, as our lives fall off,
a gull lifts us, drops us on the rocks, bare
because the tide is out. Flesh sifts the sludge.
At sea bottom, on the rocks below the wharf,
a salt foot, too humble to have a voice,
thumps for representation, joy.

Krill

The red fisherman
stands in the waters of the Sound,
then whirls toward an outer reef.
The krill and kelp spread out,
it is the sea anemone that displays the of,
the into, the within.
He throws the net about himself
as the sea breaks over him.
The krill in the net and out of it
follow him. He is almost awash
in silver and gold.
How much time has passed.
He believes the undulation of krill
leads to a world of less grief,
that the dorsal of your smelt,
your sardine, your whitebait, humped
against the ocean's spine, cheers it
in its purpose.
The krill break loose, plunge down
like a great city of lights. He is left
with the sea that he hears
with its *if* and *then*, *if* and *then*, *if* and *then*.

Peace

The trade of war is over, there are no more battles,
but simple murder is still in.
The No God, Time, creeps his way,
universe after universe, like a great snapping turtle
opening its mouth, wagging its tongue
to look like a worm or leech
so deceived hungry fish, every living thing
swims in to feed. Quarks long for dark holes,
atoms butter up molecules, protons do unto neutrons
what they would have neutrons do unto them.
The trade of war has been over so long,
the meaning of war in the O.E.D. is now "nonsense."
In the Russian Efron Encyclopedia,
war, voina, means "dog shit";
in the Littré, guerre is "a verse form, obsolete";
in Germany, Krieg has become "a whipped-cream pastry";
Sea of Words, the Chinese dictionary,
has war, zhan zheng, as "making love in public,"
while war in Arabic and Hebrew, with the same
Semitic throat, harb and milchamah, is defined
as "anything our distant grandfathers ate
we no longer find tempting—like the eyes of sheep."
And lions eat grass.

Frog

I hold this living coldness,
this gland with eyes, mouth, feet,
shattered mirror of all creatures,
pulsing smile of fish, serpent and man,
feet and hands come out of a head
that is also a tail,
just as I caught him most of my life ago
in the sawdust of the icehouse.
I could not believe in him if he were not here.
He rests my spirit
and is beautiful as waterlilies.
The sound of his call is too large for his body:
"irrelevant, irrelevant, irrelevant."
Once in the dry countries he was a god.

Vanitas

In the sideview mirror of my car
through the morning fog I saw a human skull
that had to be my face, where the headlights
of the car behind me should have been,
or a morning star. I did not think
to step on the gas and race away from the skull
I knew wasn't behind me. Still it had me by the throat.
I can tell a raven from a crow,
a female evergreen from a male,
but I can't tell visionary bone from ghost.
I'm used to my eyes fibbing to me,
5s are sometimes 8s, 2s, 3s.
I know the Chinese character for the word "nature"
is a nose that stands for breathing—life.
I need to see an ancient nose in the mirror.

Lost Daughter

I have protected the flame of a match
I lit and then discarded
more than I cared for you.
I had little to go on:
a postcard that came for no reason,
forty years ago,
that told me of your birth and name,
but not who was your father.
I would never give
my child your name.
In the woods and ditches of my life you
are less than a wildflower.
If you have a garden I
am less than melted snow.
I never held your hand
and this is the only bedtime story
I will ever tell you.
No love, no prayer, no flame.

Beauty is Not Easy

What are they but cattle, these butterflies,
their purple hides torn by barbed wire,
Chinese peacock butterflies,
scarred blue, yellow and scarlet.
If they are not marked for slaughter
I cannot tell to whom they belong.
They are just stray cattle, swallowtails
The sun does not witness,
the clouds do not testify.
Beauty does not need a public defender,
but I would listen to a serious defense
of beauty—tell me what happens to the carcass,
the choice cuts, everything useful:
hide, bones, intestines, fat.
Then talk to me of butterflies.

Moss, 1987, West Shokan NY

Walking

1.

His stride is part delusion.
They laugh at him, "A little water in the boot,
he thinks he walks on water."
At home to get a cup of coffee
he walks across Norway, and his talk—
sometimes he speaks intimately to crowds,
and to one person as to a crowd. On principle
he never eats small potatoes.
Illusion, mirage, hallucination,
he loves a night painting of a fable: a man
is grinning at a boy lighting a candle from an ember,
a monkey on his shoulder chained to heaven—
a reminder that art apes nature.
When they told him "reality is simply what is,"
it was as though he had climbed Sinai,
then walked down to get the laws.
He dreams only of the migrations of peoples
beneath the migrations of birds,
he wakes to new nations, he yawns
riddles of the north and south wind,
whistles his own tune in the Holy Sepulchre.
Some afternoons he stretches out in a field
like an aqueduct. "All we do," he says,
"is carry a bucket or two of God's waters
from place to place."

2.

Under a roof, from a chandelier, on a rope,
hangs an amusing tragedy, a kind of satyr play,
but not every fat man dancing by
is wrapped in grape leaves. Facing himself
in a bronze mirror like the one
the ancient Chinese thought cured insanity,

tongue-tied he speaks to his own secret face,
or standing in the sunlight
against the lives of mountains, sky and sea,
he speaks, made-up and masked, the lyrical truth,
the bare-faced lie. Not speaking
the language of his fathers,
a hero may die because all flesh is grass
and he forgets the password.

From a lectern, or the top of a hay wagon,
or leaping down,
a few steps away from everyday life,
into something like a kitchen garden,
he unearths in the wordless soil
things sung or said, kinds of meaning:
what is denoted or symbolic,
or understood only by its music,
or caught on to without reason,
the endless twisting of its roots, its clarity.
He points to the old meaning of looking
to the Last Judgment,
while he believes nothing is merely or only.

3.

At a garden party he almost said,
"Madame, it is not in the bones of a lover or a dog
to wait long as the bleached mollusk
on the mountain. Time is an ice cube melting
in a bowl, the world is refracted, ridiculous.
In life, you often reach out for a stone
that isn't where you see it in the stream."
But it was summer,
no one would believe time was so cold
on a hot day, so comforting,
when the purple iris was already dry
and the tulips fallen.

Prayer

Give me a death like Buddha's. Let me fall
over from eating mushrooms Provençale,
a peasant wine pouring down my shirtfront,
my last request not a cry but a grunt.
Kicking my heels to heaven, may I succumb
tumbling into a rosebush after a love
half my age. Though I'm deposed, my tomb
shall not be empty; may my belly show above
my coffin like a distant hill, my mourners come
as if to pass an hour in the country,
to see the green, that old anarchy.

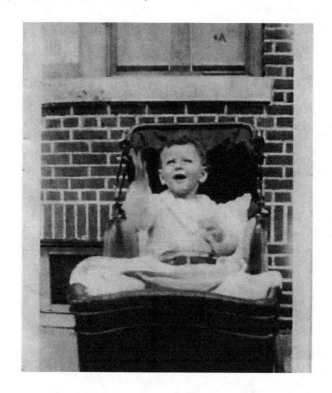

Author, aged nine months

Song of Alphabets

When I see Arabic headlines
like the wings of snakebirds,
Persian or Chinese notices
for the arrival and departures of buses—
information beautiful as flights of starlings,
I cannot tell vowel from consonant,
the sign of the vulnerability of the flesh
from signs for laws and government.

The Hebrew writing on the wall
is all consonants, the vowel
the ache and joy of life
is known by heart. There are words
written in my blood I cannot read.
I can believe a cloud gave us the laws,
parted the Red Sea, gave us the flood,
the rainbow. A cloud teaches kindness,
be prepared for the worst wind, be light of spirit.
Perhaps I have seen His cloud,
an ordinary mongrel cloud
that assumes nothing, demonstrates nothing,
that comforts as a dog sleeping in a room,
a presence offering not salvation
but a little peace.

My hand has touched the ancient Mayan God
whose face is words: a limestone beasthead
of flora, serpent and numbers,
the sockets of a skull I thought were vowels.
Hurray for English, hidden miracles,
the A and E of waking and sleeping,
the O of mouth.

Thank you, Sir, alone with your name,
for the erect L in love and open-legged V,
the beautiful Tree of Words in the forest
beside the Tree of Souls, lucky the bird
that held Alpha or Omega in his beak.

Delmore Schwartz

He heard God coughing in the next apartment,
his life a hospital, he moved from bed to bed
with us and Baudelaire, except he always had
Finnegans Wake tucked in his pajamas,
which must mean, sure as chance,
the human race is God's Phlegm. Penitent,
I say a prayer in God's throat:
"Mister, whose larynx we congest,
spit us into the Atlantic or Hudson . . .
let us be dropped into the mouth of the first fish
that survived by eating its young—
drink hot tea and honey Your mother brings You
till You are rid of Your catarrh, well again.
Let us swim back to our handiwork."

Far from the world of Howth Castle, Delmore died
in a bed-bugged hotel unclaimed for three days.
A week before, by chance, I saw him
at a drugstore counter, doubled over a coffee,
he moaned, "Faithful are the wounds of a friend,
deceitful enemy kisses."
He held my hand too tight, too long.
Melancholy Eros flew to my shoulder,
spoke in Greek, Yiddish, and English:
"Wear his sandals, his dirty underwear,
his coat of many colors that did not keep him warm."

Visiting Star

I woke at sunrise,
fed my dogs, Honey and Margie –
to the east a wall of books and windows,
a lawn, the trees in my family,
the donkeys and forest behind the hill.
Sunlight showed itself in,
passed the China butterflies on the window
so birds watch out, don't break their necks.
On the back of a green leather chair for guests
facing me in sunlight and shadow, a sunlit Star of David,
two large hand spans square.
I call my wife to see the star
she first thinks I painted on the chair.
Soon she catches on – no falling star.
We searched the room and outside.
How did the star come to be?
Without explanation. None.
The star visited a few minutes, disappeared,
or became invisible. Why?
I wondered if it was le bel aujourd'hui
or a holiday some Jews celebrate.
Playing fair, I told myself: watch out for
a crucifix anywhere before which
contrition saves condemned souls –
watch in the forest for portraits of the Virgin,
the wheel of Dharma down the road,
that teaches 'save all living beings',
when the moon is full a crescent moon
reflected on a wall or lake.
Watch for flying horses!
I read the news of commandments broken.
Thou shalt not kill.
I write between the lines

Thou shalt not steal
seventy-five years from the life of a child.
Next day, I found my Star of David
was a glass sun and star reflection of
a tinkling shimmering wind chime made in China.
A pleasing, godless today fills my study.

Clouds

Two beautiful women in the sky kissing,
their arms and legs wrapped around each other,
one has wings, is an angel. Her lover's left hand
is deep in her feathers. Her lover's right hand
reaches deep inside her. Their tongues
are pink, gentle, rough or hard.
The miracle is that a cloud can kiss,
that if one cloud has wings and is wrapped
around the other, the other is helpless.
Now they are rolling over each other.
I wish I could carve 'Stanley'
on the white marble bluff. I am in Cardiff.
I sleep at the Angel Hotel.

They Plow Their Father's Field

I taught English poetry in Beijing
30 years ago. I thought
there has to be a special name
for Chinese work,
working the same field
in the same way with the same
wooden implement, the plow
looked Chinese 8000 years ago.

The shape of a character in calligraphy
is not work or labor or farming or plowing—
is part study, part poetry.
The character for truth is a real theory.
For the name of a girl,
a dead poet's daughter,
the character is plain
the name means she is a commoner.
Her brother is Sho-fan, Sunshine,
he is a poet who
works for Tel and Tel.
Both children are often lonely.
Their surname Yang means Flute.
They are their mother's joy,
they plow their father's field.

—To He Huaren

Li Hua (b. 1907) woodblock, 1947.

The Grammarian

I say, to be silly,
Death is a grammarian.
He needs the simple past,
the *passato remoto*, the *passé composé*,
the *le* in Chinese added
to any verb in the present
that makes it past.
In the pluperfect houses of worship
death hangs around,
is thought to be undone.
Sometimes he is welcome.
I thank him for the simple present
and his patience.

For My Godmother, Twenty Years Later

Give me a death like hers without tears,
those flies on a summer day about a carcass—
about the house medicine, Mozart, and good cheer.
My song: life is short, art long, death longer.
My doctor uncle covered her with kisses.
When her life was a goldfinch in his hand,
on a feeder and birdbath outside her window:
larks sang, splashed and fed above the sparrows.
A blue jay militaire drove them away.
Then, a bird of prey, a necessary reprimand
screamed overhead without mercy. Instead
of terror, it was met at her window
by the warbler of good cheer that sometimes sings for the dead.
I whistle for it to come and nest near my window.

March 21st, First Day of Spring

Twenty inches of snow on the ground,
I saw a swallow with a blade of dry grass
begin to build a nest on my porch
between an American Corinthian capital
and a gutter, where he or she nests every year.
Welcome, welcome! What can I do to help?
I'll stay in my warm house, get out of your way,
I'll watch out for raccoons, and eagles.
I leave apples on the porch, seeds in a bucket.
Where have you been all winter?
I know Welsh swallows winter in Egypt.
It makes me shudder to think you fly south
from the Catskills to the Andes.
The important thing is you're back.
Suddenly I am in the arms of spring.
I love you but don't know if you're a mother
or a father bird. I feel safe with you here.
I think I'll write the Times: better your nest
than a flock of aircraft carriers in the harbor.

Pax Poetica

The earth needs peace more than it needs the moon,
that beauty without which the oceans lose their intellect.
Peace in bombed gardens where butterflies swoon
into the sun, living one day and dying in the shelling
of that night, where joyous rat and knife inspect
the numerous wares the dead are selling.
The earth needs peace more than it needs the moon.
Sometimes the dead lie hand in hand: six, seven, eight
after a night of minuses and endless decrease,
they do not serve, or stand or wait,
they unpeople themselves flogged in the sun.
No caesura. No rainbow. No peace.
I pity the poets who think that war will be undone
by poetry, the hate-filled world saved by music. I am one. . .
A little more time and poetry will set things straight.
It took time to find the Golden Fleece.
The useless dead hang in markets of the sun,
alone as pork thighs. Every morning comes and goes
more quickly. I know where wild thyme blows,
that naked beauty steals naked to my arms, then goes
to pay a debt to sorrow. No peace.
In a sometime-sometime land, there will be no joy in killing.
We are meant to hold each other but not for keeping;
we kill—just as the toad cannot keep from leaping.
In the grave there is no work or device
nor knowledge nor wisdom, I read in Ecclesiastes.
Still, fishermen lift their nets, hoist death weeping,
throw back death twinkling like a small coin into the profitless seas.
Look, the eternal fish swims away leaping.
Moonless, we still have starlight, the aurora borealis,
fires above the Conqueror Worm and beneath
till the sun runs off with the earth in its teeth.

My History of Laughter

My history of laughter:
the first human beings who laughed
were thrown out of their caves by grunters
and humpers because they wanted romance.
Chuckles and smiles. There must have been laughter
before marriage vows and last rites.
"We are the only mammals who laugh" is not true.
There are those who laugh a lot
because of too much grief.
Every living thing laughs.
Flowers laugh so hard their petals fall.
Gardens are sometimes like a theatre
with comic and tragic hydrangeas,
some roses have thorns.
I hear laughter, it's raining hard,
laughter after a hot summer day.
If you don't think maples, oaks, evergreens laugh,
walk in another part of the forest,
come sit with me under a greenwood tree.
I smile when I hear "War of the Roses," laugh
with the laughing birds: the green woodpeckers,
laughing thrush, laughing doves and crows.
I am a bird feeder, a laugh,
some birds hunt for dead men's teeth.

Beautiful to think in the beginning was the word
according to Matthew, according to Mark,
according to John, according to Luke. I play
the most Christian instrument: the accordion.
(I hear a little laughter in the pit). Further back,
when the Spirit of God moved on the face of the waters,
when God created the heavens and the earth
laughter came about the time there was light,
laughter and light were good. Jokes become comics.

Tonight, come and kiss me sweet and sixty
seventy, eighty, ninety.
I sing a song of my devotion,
I'm a little drunk, be my ocean,
take me on a cruise
around the world. Be my muse,
show me poetry is not complaining,
the truest poetry is the most feigning.
Ocean, come over my bow, let's sail
Into the fog up ahead, the future.
Kind winds prevail,
there is no end, there is departure.
Night comes. I sound a foghorn,
I am reborn.
I'm beginning to know who I am,
I want. I give a damn.
Darling ocean, sweet adventure,
I am a gardener, a rake, the grand tour.
Youth's a stuff will not endure.

Wordsworth beheld "the sea lay laughing at a distance."
If water equals time, providing beauty with its double,
so be it. I keep time with water clocks,
Greek and medieval candle clocks.
I know how to make a laughing clock:
ha, haha, hahaha, up to twelve.
I want this verse to be a laughing clock.
I have not forgotten the sun on water
is a ripple of laughter.
In a confession booth a sinner
laughed so piously he was given absolution.
He did not hail Mary, he laughed with her.
Freud on humor: A man about to be hanged
says, What a beautiful day for a hanging.

A newborn sinless babe does not laugh.
A world away from The Book of Proverbs,
the Japanese have a saying, "Letting off a fart
doesn't make you laugh when you are alone." Idle
reader, I never heard a snake break wind.
A rattlesnake did a twisting dance in my
house. I picked up the serpent with two sticks,
threw it into an apple tree. It didn't get the joke,
went off without enchantment in search of a charmer.

Here is my fairy tale, The Birthday Cake:
you take six eggs, beat the yolks and whites,
a little flour, half an hour in the oven.
Laughter. The batter rises,
strawberries and cream for shortcake.
A loving mother hen missed her eggs,
she jumped on top of the cake, sat on her beaten eggs,
wept on the pretty cake in the center of the table.
Outside in the yard a rooster mounted
a New Hampshire Red. The guests laughed.

I circled Manhattan with Pablo Neruda
on a ferry—Neruda, Communist rooster
on top of the world, dressed, it seemed,
in Savile Row tweed, Church's shoes. We talked.
He remembered under the Triboro Bridge,
"I asked Lorca to come with me to a circus:
old tightrope walkers and acrobats,
an old clown shot out of a cannon."
Lorca's answered a 1935 question
with an Andalusian frown that suffers in translation,
"Pablo, it's getting difficult. I must leave España,
go to Granada to kiss the Lorcas and Romeros goodbye."
Federico was shot by unnecessary bullets
that whistled half notes and quarter notes.

He died at sunrise, not five o'clock
in the afternoon. Fascist laughter.

Present mirth has present laughter.
Buddha laughs with joy, thanks to the hereafter.
Someone shouts, "There is the laughter of murderers!
Nothing funnier than a dead body!"
It's worth repeating: *170 pounds of cold meat,*
four buckets of water, a pocket of salt.
I throw my sombrero into the Mediterranean.
It floats—mysterious laughter.
I can see Silenus laughing with Dionysus.
They drink laughing wine in dazzling goblets.
I can't forget Eros laughs with happy lovers
in cheap, dear rooms of Washington Heights.

I remember a Bernini fountain, in Piazza Navona,
water laughing, I drank out of the mouth of a satyr.
The satyr kissed me.
It was Epiphany, when shepherds come to Rome
from the *compagna*, playing goatskin bagpipes.
When I'm laid out, I prefer to keep my skin.
They can make a bagpipe fashioned of my laughing belly,
I'll be a musical instrument, I prefer
being blown than fingered like a harp or clavier.

I was moved to tears by a laughing jazz band,
black laughter instead of drums. Chick Webb could do it,
Louis Armstrong forced a scat-laugh revolution.
Laughter is ancient as the sun, older than the moon.
The Chinese word for laughter is made of two characters:
the character for sky beneath the character for grass.

Translated in Chinese a laughing Falstaff
might give you a dancing Falstaff tripping on a sunset,
upside down cows and sheep grazing in the sky.
What is the moon doing rising below my feet?
Laugh me to scorn.
"Weeping may endure all night,
but joy cometh in the morning."

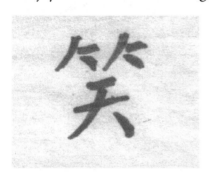

Not Yet
Poems August 2020 – May 2021

Not Yet

These days I regret less. There are questions
of memory, acts of forgetfulness.
When Odysseus went underground
to meet his mother who was a shade,
he tried to hug her.
He embraced a fleshless remembrance.
Mandelstam wrote his poems in his head
walking around St. Petersburg and Moscow.
When he got home, he inscribed his poems.
What more could he do in lying times?
He had Homer and Russian orioles in his head.
There is a species of human beings
who read ten pages of prose, often regretfully,
can't help remember every word.
Britten wrote *A Midsummer Night's Dream*,
before he set down a note. Inexplicable
music and opera are the father and mother,
the lyrics a child who plays with vowels,
slides and swings, until the composer mother
calls her child to supper, where they say grace.
Memory is thankful, I regret my unthankfulness.
I've walked into an ocean. In D minor
Bach wrote a Concerto for 3 piano keyboards.
I want to speak like a concerto
for 3 pianos to green readers in D minor,
and readers who know they will die soon.
They deserve attention.

A Smiling Understanding

There is an understanding,
a smiling understanding,
between orchards and orchestras.
Jazz and Bach are fertilizers,
something extra. Trees are much older than music
and poetry. They have bodies and souls,
godlike identities. Trees are choirs,
basso profundos, coloraturas, mezzo sopranos.
I live with music and trees, orchards of music,
woodwinds and sextets. I sing
the "I don't lie to myself" blues.
I learn from my suffering to understand
the suffering of others. I climb musical scales.
Trees have an embouchure. I'm a sapling.
Breath and wind blow through me.
This winter is a coda of falling leaves,
sequoias and maples Louis Armstrong.
I have a band of tree brothers and sisters,
we are not melancholy babies.
I age like a rock, not a rocking chair.
A rock does not wear spectacles, hearing aids,
or use a walking stick. It is dangerous
for anyone to call me "young fellow."

Today is Yesterday, Tomorrow and Now

Sitting alone, having my morning coffee,
I have a young body, one foot on the table,
to make it easy for my heart to pump
blood throughout me to my brain.
I am convinced I have a young body.

A beautiful red-headed Irish lady
is coming Wednesday
to discover her literary future.
She has a passion for Irish poetry.
She's forty, has not written a poem.
There's a future for her body and soul,
mine too. How does she smell and feel,
touched intellectually, then by a hand?

I'm sure I have a long, sinful future.
I'm sinful as an apple tree I love
that I planted ten years ago,
close to my back porch where I lie half-naked.
I think my thoughts clean up millimeters
of smog from the air the world is breathing.

I live in an always, always land,
where just as hummingbird wings
flutter a hundred times a second,
I visit, I'm there, soon as I name someplace
I don't have to pronounce in my head,
I'm at Piazza di Spagna, Place des Vosges,
the temple of the vestigial virgins,
Delphi, St. Martin In The Fields. I've seen
a beautiful bird for every heartbeat I've had.
What will a beautiful Irish lady think of that?

She came, most of her Irish accent gone.
What a pity. For 20 minutes
there were smiles and thank yous
for information and teaching.
Her voice was American Catskill plain.
In minutes she was gone.
Mad Ireland, I want to have you, know you.
I'm cultivated as a glass of water.
I'm tempted to say out loud to myself,
"I feel pretty good: silly and stupid."
Today is yesterday, tomorrow and now.
I'm immortal as a squirrel who thinks
I am a bystander, sometimes an enemy.
Life everlasting is possible, look at
the sun and a clouded sky. If there aren't
dogs in the afterlife, I'll stay here.

Dog Sonnet

My dogs won't let anyone sit in my chair
when I'm away a few days for business
or medical reasons. When I am 10 miles away,
coming home, they run to the back door
and wait for me. They know I belong to them.
Truth is, Margie doesn't understand prose.
She wants me to bark back at her for fun and love.
I wish the word "bark" had the sound of barking.
The word "rough" sounds like a bark.
Rough, rough, rough, rough, rough.
The truth is, I do bark and growl at Margie,
as I do at my readers.
Could I write a growling sonnet?
I love you, growl, is an affectionate line.

After Receiving a Letter

At home now with his wife Prue, hoping,
the armada Covid-19 will shipwreck,
the poet John Fuller spends valuable time
washing and ironing stains and wrinkles
out of sheets, shirts, and blouses,
intimate cloth not just collars and cuffs.
He knows English wool, not Irish linen,
shrinks in dangerous hot water,
once the English insisted the anointed Irish
shroud their dead in English wool, not Irish linen.

The oceans have been doing our washing
since the beginning, the sun does the ironing.
Oceans must clean up, mop the coastlines
with water we dirty with human waste,
bilge: plastics, bottles, and petroleum.
"No crabs and eels in my washing machine,"
some politicians are proud to say.

Lovingly, poets can wash and iron a sonnet,
its feet and rhymes, hear and count each line
fourteen times. Finding truth is not ironing
around buttons. The truth cut off by an iron
is not a button, cannot be sewed back on.
A fact can be cut off, sewed back on.
A button of truth is never a zipper.
I'd bet my life the Fullers' garden and house
smells to high heaven of love and poetry.

I Write to Be Read Out Loud

You will never find the word moon
placed high right on my page
as if a page is sky and earth,
below halfway down circles of Hell.
I write to be read out loud by someone alone,
or in a theater with standing room only.
No page is a field with sheep grazing
no skyscrapers, no bridges.
There is the history of punctuation,
sometimes punctuation murders the dead
with colons and semi-colons. I draw in my notebook
weeping willows, flowers, faces next to poems.
My mother told me the sun sleeps close to me.
I will die with the speed of light.
I'm in the wrong lane
I crash, slam on the emergency brake.
I have four flat tires, good health. I'm out of ink.
I write with my index finger on stone.
You think stone is a blank page; it's not.
There's a moon on my swollen left foot
that is a corn on my pinky toe.
I have high arches, not flat feet,
two triumphant arches, still I limp.
Now I'm almost at the bottom of the page.
Fireworks, music, celebrating life.
I can make a face in a rage at death with full stops.

I Miss Naomi Étienne

I miss Naomi Étienne.
She's back on St. Lucia
to claim her inheritance 10 years late,
an angel in flight, she needs to escape
my devilish demands that she wear a mask.
I ache to hear the beautiful music
her highly intelligent patois,
her lively ungrammatical English speech.
She thinks according to the Bible,
"God made Covid-19."
Her superstition is a work of art.
Her church in Brooklyn has a congregation
six nurses domestic workers, their Sabbath
is Friday and Saturday until sunset.
Her pastor supports his family and others
by his labors in construction.
Lord, why are job and Job
spelled the same in English —
surely not in Greek or Hebrew.
Naomi doesn't celebrate Christmas
on the 25th of December because
"Jesus wasn't born on a Roman holiday,"
but the Roman emperor Augustus' mother
found Christ's grave in 300 A.D
where the church of the resurrection stands.
What the hell, that's not in the Hebrew Bible,
if all the world's a bar and not a stage,
Naomi prefers with her salmon's head, margaritas.
I'll take rum from St Lucia.
We dance together at weddings.

I'm Sorry
To W.H. Auden

I'm sorry, exhausted, except for funds.
I wrote a check, the date October 18
without the year, to Theresa Monrose
for a hundred dollars, I did not write
the amount longhand.
My conversation with friends
is something like the way I wrote that check
when I try to tell what I owe them.
I don't get it right, I leave off years,
the everyday debt made clear by saying
something like thank you,
in a handwritten letter.
Yes, I believe everyone's
time of day or night is different.
I'm sure a poet I love,
who demanded punctuality,
never bounced a check.
When he died, age 66,
at the Altenburgerhof Hotel,
he did not pay his bill.
I guarantee the world will pay
for his empty zimmer a hundred years.
I can't get Siegfried's Funeral March out of my ears.

Looney Tune

I'll see you soon
is a looney tune
friends and lovers are far away
shaking hands is a no no
shake your head yes or no instead.
It's deathly to love a stranger
close enough to hear her or him
masked and speaking to you.
A year of this loneliness
is like a thirty years war, the religious
and atheists are on a sorrow go round.
Walking alone on Madison Avenue,
in Harlem or Washington Heights,
or any country Main Street
everything closed, boarded up.
For company I hear myself whistle
a looney tune: I'll see you soon.
Passing a nailed shut art gallery
I think of Di Chirico's town squares
with a distant statue, but no people,
ancient Rome in the wee hours.
If the ocean floods a graveyard
the dead are salty;
they may set sail out of their graves
into the branches, the open arms of a tree.
I would be pleased to be embraced by a tree.
I'm singing my looney tune.
I'll salt tax you again,
I somersault, it pleases me.
I am a naked clown,
I ring your music hall doorbell.
you ask "who's there?",
afraid I will assault you,
when I want to exalt you.
Yesterday was the last day of summer,

600,000 died in the USA
unnecessarily, while friends in the sunset
far west battle in a no man's land
of forest fires. Wildlife
animals, insects, and human beings
burn alive with masked firemen and women,
160 million trees ashes,
songbirds are screaming,
ashes everywhere. It's ash Thursday,
Friday, Saturday, Sunday, Monday,
Tuesday and Ash Wednesday.
Choking on smoke from fires
3,000 miles away. I take one word
from the arithmetic of disaster,
multiply and square root it,
I learn the mathematics
of a sentence. I add up and divide,
I read and write. Outside my locked door
and windows is my three thousand mile
fire escape. I want to see you soon, perhaps
I'll see you when 10 times 10 is not 100,
because no number one is equal to another one,
except when one plus one makes a happy two.
*   *   *

Today I saw a life loving grasshopper
among my Buddhist flowers,
far from the totalitarian locusts
that devour cultivated fields,
winter and summer wheat, corn, living greenery,
red strawberries, black and blue berries, sunflowers.
Every locust has a formal education:
laurel is a bush not a tree.
Like father like son, the apple does not fall
far from the tree
except if the tree is on a hill, the apple may roll
downhill into the sea or river.
A wise carp eats that apple. I hope

a vegetarian carp will read to me.
Looney?
I was brought up in a madhouse.
Anything brought up in the ocean is salty.
The living brought up in a happy home
may know happiness without ever being happy.
He or she may simply be a passenger
not part of the ship's crew.
I was a farmer in the city, far from a farm.
There are church women and men who never go to church.
I consider there are male and female giants,
John Keats was five foot three.
Inside my wine glass there may be sand.
In a giant coffin I've seen a murdered infant
buried, a black baby in a white adult coffin.

Summer ended two days ago. On my farm
there was a frost last night. The seasons think...
I give human characteristics to time and space,
who are grandparents of mother nature.
I am reasonable,
I love beauty that happened:
Pope Julius II hired Raphael to paint
time and space as people, men and women
who go to mass, the Church triumphant.
Further back the Greeks wrote of Corinthian, Doric,
Ionic columns as a "family."

I choose to give *I'll see you soon* toothpicks
to the moon that has no teeth.
On a dark night I heard the moon sing
I'll see you soon, a song without music
or words.
I want to be buried in song
without music or words, with ashes I saved
eight loved dogs at my feet.

There is Secret Meaning in Rhymes

There's a secret meaning in rhymes,
a wish to discover the unknown sometimes:
robin, sin, bird, word, absurd,
repent, serpent, disobedient.
Such rhymes make a flock,
they don't make a poem
in London, Paris, or Rome,
reason is a key that does not fit a lock.

I'm out of season, the reason I sigh:
rhyme is a way of saying goodbye.
I know my summer heart's becoming winter ice,
laughter or weeping is not a choice,
it's all in what's called the heart and the voice.
No may mean yes, everybody's no may mean yes.
Every rhyme welcomes a good friend,
English prosody has no likeness.
Some rhymes are forced, raped in the end,
by a liar who lies to himself and other liars.
Give them sandwiches wrapped in barbed wire.
A forced rhyme is a lie, a libel,
a crime, the Gods and my friends offended,
a poet's hand is always on a Bible,
or another sacred Godly scribble.

The earth is harmonious,
two-thirds musical saltwater.
W. B. Yeats had a beautiful daughter.
Everyday I'm thankful, not jealous,
of his vital life, a house ceremonious,
disgraced by his love for dictatorial slaughter.
I am secular, pagan and religious.
Saint Teresa of Avila married Jesus
and the poet San Juan de la Cruz.
Not telling the truth, rhyme may tell the truth.

There's music in every word, a secret
there's a secret in every rhyme, a duet
a Liebestod, a Romeo and Juliet.

Contra Goya

Traveler sleep,
take your Time,
you have never been
where skeletons have dominion.
Given war, plagues,
old age and accidents,
the boatmen never sleeps.
Even the most experienced
gondoliers – after weddings,
funerals, the Feast
of the Epiphany,
Easter – are drowsy.
They sleep, protected from weather
under a bridge of thundering feet.
After a revolution
anywhere "Time is,"
I heard the boatman sing,
"The dream, the sleep of reason,
produces angels."

A Rum Cocktail

I'm in France, happily a little drunk in Nice.
The barman mixes rum with lime
strained through cracked ice.
He says he's an actor most of the time,
he has 20 lines in a verse play, *The Absurd*.
He fills my glass, some thoughts die, some endure,
he scratches what I'm not supposed to notice,
challenging the actor is a poet's pleasure,
lives change for the better, for good measure,
if the play is great...I, Stanley, give you my word,
my heroes will not repent a theatrical truth,
an upstage truth. I drink "to life,"
I don't applaud Mary in a confession booth.
The barges and cafes along the Rhone
are far from the *Bateau Ivre*. This *apéritif*
is a call to my arms on a telephone.
The poem of self is undone and done,
I've made a lock without a key. Whatever I do
I'm locked into what's new,
a necessary pebble, not a granite rock in my shoe.
Infancy is very slow, old age is fast.
Not manneristic, I had porridge for breakfast,
my memory is like a Cubist fresco
in chambre 10 at the Hotel Negresco.
My continuing joy since I was young
Picasso's *Demoiselles d'Avignon*,
my friendship and love for Miró and Rothko.
However beautiful the day, there's sorrow,
I leave for *España Negra* tomorrow,
mis amores, on the *Ramblas de Las Flores*.

The Inconsequential, a Paper Napkin

These days we are expelled into the world,
naked from a life of dreams,
or a life where the living never sleep,
into a world we will in time recognize.

Everything since the Virus seems inconsequential:
what is, was, or might once have been
beloved or despised, the enchanting,
the always, the never, the occasional,
the singular, the most extraordinary, the commonplace,
the boring, the least and most suffering
at great distances and differences,
are now or are becoming inconsequential.

Still there is breathing in and out,
plus other necessities, the luxury of concerns:
our loves, the sink, faucets, and drains,
the lost, found, and misplaced,
the streets shut down or almost empty,
windows boarded up. The afterlife
desired by most of us is a given.
I'm willing to have faith that bacteria fighting for life
have equivalent churches, synagogues, mosques,
temples, monasteries, nunneries.
A microbe has laws, but no holy books.

Why don't I write a fable: *Twice Upon a Time*,
there will be a democratic election.
May the election lights shine on those
who think truth and kindness matter. I see a wonderland,
I can't watch the Republican Convention on TV.
I choose Olivier's *Lear, Henry V, Othello*
thanks to CDs. For the fun of it, I boast.
I can hold my silence longer than Iago.
This verse is a handkerchief

that was my mother's gift to me.
She thought it was a paper napkin
to wipe my mouth, keep it clean.

I tighten both my fists. I won't let go.
I'll write a leaflet of last words.
I cough and spit blood,
I take my finger and make a flower of blood and spit:
a howling wild rose.
I undress the statue of liberty.
Now she stands naked in the harbor,
requesting the tired, the poor,
the huddled masses.

The Legend of Self 2021
to Louise Glück

The poem of the imagined self,
Kunitz's "legend of self,"
the unimaginable self,
the poem of who you are,
were. The poem of self, singular,
plural, still exists.

You invented an eight year old brother.
I had 3 brothers. Father traveled,
promoting history books he and others wrote,
translated into half a dozen languages.
So I have a Mexican-American brother
who writes poetry, literary history,
novels, translations. He's a don at Cambridge.
No place, no place in the world,
does he love more than Oaxaca.
He knows languages better
than rivers and railway stations.
Thanks to DNA he's straight and gay,
never crooked. His ID is books.

"All the world's a stage,"
sometimes a written page,
a bad joke. Life is a bad
joke, painful as crucifixion.
An Anglican, I'm not sure
if he believes in resurrection.
He respects Christopher Wren,
architectural erections,
the other kind he salutes.
A margarita for your thoughts,
margaritas are daisies in Rome.
I'm getting hoarse, it's hard for me to speak.
I close my mouth, take a deep breath,

think of poetry in English, French, Spanish,
German, Portugese, without translation.
I miss the boat in several languages
so I fall into the ocean of poetry.
I can swim.

My other brother I speak to on the phone
every week, hours, these sixty years.
I read my poems, the senseless, the bad, the good,
the inconsequential, musical grub played on.
God forgive me, I once read him a poem
when he was on a dentist's chair.
He has children, part Chinese, part Greek,
part Jewish, 2 parts French,
2 parts Spanish. He's a salad.
Every day is a salad day to him.
His children have a Greek mother,
he has a Corinthian architect son,
a Doric poet daughter. He has a son
who is a broken mirror of his father,
put together with Delphic crazy glue,
roses, lilac, a little honey.
The word honey makes me remember
my dog, Honey, a sweetheart beyond words.
If I could bark like her, my poetry
would be close to truth.
Truth doesn't seem a good name for a dog,
but Honey never lied. She loved to be kissed by me.
She loved what and whom she loved,
had a way of ignoring, or being absolutely indifferent
to the rest. She appreciated human conversation,
the wonderful bitch, Mother Nature,
poetry read out loud, music,
the smell of cooking, raw meat.
Truth is, we're not body and soul
we are soul and raw meat. I don't sell raw meat.

Embrace my raw meat, cook me a little if you like.
I am yours, underdone.
Leave some of me for tomorrow
and the day after. Smell me,
touch my raw meat. I have a voice,
I'll sing to you. Raw meat is naked,
doesn't wear bedroom slippers.
I am my own brother, father, mother, and sister.
Hello there, and goodbye here and there.
Truth is, I am an unpaid worker, I wander.
On pay day, I die.

Cake Mistake

Jane made a little mistake:
taken by a Mozart serenade,
she dropped her hearing aid
in a leftover chocolate cake.
She couldn't find it for five days.
The cake couldn't hear,
it has no ear.
A cake has a life
no husband or wife,
A cake has its ways on birthdays and holidays.
Who else bleeds chocolate when cut with a knife,
avoids conversation with a cantaloupe
in the fridge with leftover soup?
Is there more angel food cake or devil's food cake?
Peace on earth is a piece of cake.
The Lord is never deaf to prayers,
He hears reasons without rhyme,
you have your God, I'll have mine.
He's having a heavenly hell of a time,
He's a good sport, He blesses poor players
for His own sake. He allows, he forgets.
Some sins are deadly, some silhouettes,
He forgives mistakes that are just wishes.
A question may shoot, and it fishes.
Do cakes have bodies and souls?
Hearing aids are God's trolls
who hear "you're guilty" as "innocent."
He is a landlord, we must pay rent.
Saint Donald of Trump was president.
Soon I believe he'll be in Trump hell,
permanently under a waterfall of golf balls.

Some Words for T.R. Hummer

Masked, I send my vulgar sympathy, ignorant gossip.
My friend had a No Thanks, No Thanks, Thanksgiving.
His mother at 96 died alone in Texas,
quarantined 2,000 miles away,
hopefully comforted by a kind stranger.
His wife, Elizabeth, broke a world record,
for a hasty, fourth stage, hard to say, breast cancer.
His wife and my wife are thankful for infusions,
we're dancing cheek to cheek in virus time.
I don't know what's doing,
his 'I' a significant presence,
with his early wife's nearby daughter.
My friend writes poetry
for every body and soul in the world.
Yes, he has a distant son at a long table.
It's a familiar story,
the ghosts of twelve fishermen have supper
with him, the conversation about good times,
music, the past, Bad Joke.
Once Bad Joke was the name
of a revolutionary slave.

Time passes on a looney calendar,
he obeyed the commandment
"music in the park." His writing hints, does not say,
"Soon I'll dine to music in silence, alone.
I'll walk down the street in peace,
20 or 30 ghosts walk with me.
I take a bath with 20 or 30 ghosts."

There's something unsanitary about death.
Most of us want a clean death
with an ashtray in our coffin.
Terry planted 10 roses in memory of his mother,

and two autumn ferns. Still, there was a garbage can full of his old life:
Terry had to throw away his bottles, breasts,
vaginas, motherlove, married life.
Now he's a teetotaler, a toddler-adolescent,
a 70 year old beginner. He will get through kindergarten
and grammar school again, skip through high school.
He must raise his hand to leave the room,
to be given new teeth, new eyes,
ears, mouth, and nose, except
when he looks in the mirror, mirrors in Mississippi
others in Gambier Ohio, Coldspring.
He has a house of books and music,
closed books and open books like his heart.
Outside the window, Mother Nature,
Father, Brother, Sister, Son, and Daughter Nature.

Keeping up appearances, he acts as if
every living thing was God who created him,
the blues, water, and stones created him.
His mother did not die. The herbivorous
and carnivorous eat dead souls,
eat your life, the automobiles of your life.
Your tears are horseless carriages,
there are ticking handless watches.
Terry will not write artificial intelligence prose,
in an age of computer music, hip hop,
first and last dances and chances.
An orchestra is not a rubber band
imprisoning a deck of cards,
the population of every town and city,
deuces and jack republicans,
kings and queens are Biblical. Jehovah,
holy Mary, no one ever wasted time
working in a garden.
His life is a memorial service for his mother.
He dials Mother 4-5-6 on the telephone.

Voicemail just beeps. I bet my life he'll refuse
to spend the rest of his life
writing elegies, singing scat hymns,
after his No Thanks, No Thanks, Thanksgiving.
Terry will still celebrate Christmas.
Jesus works for a federal minimum wage
of seven dollars and fifty cents an hour.

Whim

There are works of God,
like Transubstantiation.
There is no common-mode current,
alternating-current God.
I think every living thing
anywhere sings, buzzes, bubbles,
rustles, something like *amour,*
roses and briars. Is this sip of thought
a frivolous introspection?
A zero plus a zero plus a zero
is not a naught. Galileo said,
"Sad is a country that needs a hero."
Many a word is thrown away
with all its frills upon it. Syllables,
beats, rhymes can make a loveless sonnet.

A Prayer to No God for Ilhan Comak

Almighty, please give some pleasure
to a Kurdish poet, prisoner, student of geography,
locked in a Turkish cell for 27 years.
I hope his cell has a window so he can see
birds, trees of some kind, occasionally
a human being, the beauty of the world.
Does he know in English, God and prison guard
sound the same? Does Allah, a prison guard, whip him?
I bless you, Lord, I'll hear your confession.
May Ilhan tell stories with happy endings
to himself. He remembers very well
the smell of good cooking. He knows a man
can be locked in his cell with his love locked out,
still the good ghost of his love lies with him
on the toilet cell floor decorated
with flowery dead defecation.
I hope he can pretend he's having good times
swimming across the Bosphorus to Asia.
Savior, give him hope if he has no hope,
give him children, a dog, a cat, toys,
the world, an imaginary toy he can play with.

Erdogan's gang is against it, but the poet retains
the freedom to speak to himself, play with himself,
sing to himself, argue with himself in Kurdish.
If giving up his principles freed him,
I think he'd refuse dirty silence.
After 27 years in a cell, would I shut up?
In prison without hearing loved music or new music,
except your own songs and whistles, is torture,
an upside down crucifixion.
I wish hell were a real place for Erdogan's mob
a place where they are all equals, so they
have the pleasure of living with themselves.

Can Ilhan read books, the Quran, now?
In the Kurdish geography of his cell,
there is Syria, the Red and Black Seas.

From my farm in Rhinebeck, New York,
in the Catskill Mountains, near the Hudson,
across the world, a man who never prays
writes this prayer for him.
I'm his friend he never met,
a Jew he will never meet.
Free, I believe Ilhan would fight to the death
for his countrymen, Kurds without a country,
live for the right to tell and write the truth,
sometimes called kindness, sometimes poetry.

Disappearance

Madrileño with native King's English,
Christopher González-Aller,
very darling friend for half my life,
disappeared for three years. I did everything
21st century possible to touch him,
to speak to him, to see him face to face
or on my stupid phone, till the other day,
out of the blue, the bluest of blues, he sent
email Christmas greetings, a painting
of roses, a Christ child and a lamb.
I emailed back a happy "what's up" letter.
No reply, he disappeared again.

Christopher, are you playing hide and seek?
Come out, come out, wherever you are.
I suspect something painful has happened,
so painful you won't share your pain
except with Christ or a darling girl or boyfriend
or both, in romantic bondage.

I risk thinking you've cloistered yourself,
taken a vow of silence in a monastery,
nunnery, or mosque, you've granted yourself
an indulgence despite your rules, allowed thyself
to send a card one ecumenical Christmas day.
Your Christmas card celebrates not a garden,
but flowers and Christ. Flowers do not have virgin
mothers, bees and wind pollinate their stigmas.
Wild roses search for a rosary, a holy father.

I offer love to you now, not nosiness.
Life is seasonal, are you a man or woman
or both, a goat, a pussycat, or hippopotamus?
I'm all of these. I'm not ashamed. Like roses,

I pollinate, you understand, I bloom.
I'm a wildflower, my dog, Margie, smells me,
understands how many identities I have.
I'm a wild nameless flower in a forest,
on a railroad track, insulted in a pot.

Don Christopher, on a mystical Christmas card
you sing *Noel, Noel* so softly and sweetly
no one can hear you, you are alone in the snow.

For reasons some call *Quixotadas,*
you spent years relaxing from Spanish taxation
at the Minzah Hotel in Tangier, Morocco,
in an apartment with a bedroom stage
where blind musicians played for lovers.
When last we spoke you were in Marrakesh
with snake charmers, listening to a redhead
lady soothsaying, predicting the future.
When I was in Marrakesh, foreigners dressed
for dinner. There was dancing, drums and death rattles.

Do you have Winston Churchill's "black dog,"
do you reread Tory Dent's wise poems,
HIV Mon Amor? Christopher,
I can still cook. I invite you and four friends
in love to a feast of the imagination.
I'll say grace, ask Pope Francis
to make Saint Christopher a Saint again.

Happy 55th Birthday to Angel, From Stanley

Dearest mortal archangel,
I throw you a happy birthday kiss
3,000 miles across the Atlantic.
I know you are loved enough
to catch my kiss in your heart or hat.
I catch your smile you throw back to me,
it tastes good, I feed it to my dog, Margie.
I owe you a birthday cake with
56 candles, one for the hell of it.
I am 40 candles older than you.
Jesus taught us to forgive our debtors.

I hope and wish, I hope and wish,
I hope and wish,
until it becomes music, a hymn:
Abide with Michael.
Love is not a drink, although
most of the world is thirsty for it.
Love is sheep or goat's milk to many,
for others, the milk of human kindness.

Some say love is a margarita,
silly lovers think it is alcoholic rum
and coca-cola. Love is a god, Eros,
who will leap from your back to Michael's
and back to you again. Weeping Aphrodite,
Orpheus, Selene, Eurydice, Poseidon,
you both are all of these gods and goddesses.
I wish you and Eros a happy birthday.
I wish I knew your favorite song, I'd sing it.
In the meantime, I clear my throat and sing:
Everyone says I love you,
the cop on the corner and the burglar too,
the preacher in the pulpit, the man in the pew,

126

says I love you.
When a lion roars, there's another lion
who knows just what he's roaring for...
Love,
Stanley

A Show

The character of people shows in how
they swim, some original strokes, crawls,
backstrokes, sometimes burlesque,
butterfly strokes with a dolphin kick.
There are boys who make a living
diving for coins off cliffs.
Babies are born swimmers
after a couple years you have to teach them
to swim again or they'll sink.

Another Birthday Poem, Written When Angel was Almost a Day Older

Sometimes I think of Angel
as a Mexican guitarist
who is a Manchester florist,
who will sell Chrysanthemums
with tortillas and rum.
When someone, perhaps Osiris,
sent the virus,
Angel closed the shop,
the truth you will adore,
he locked the angel of death in the store.
Suddenly death produces laughter,
I told him man to man
I'm climbing the ladder of poetry after
you, stop devouring every living thing
with eyes, arms, private parts, antennae, wings.
Once we were the angel of death's lollipop,
now he's locked in Angel's flower shop
forever, or until every acorn is a tree.
In Hebrew, the angry angel of death
yanks out one by one
the eye and tongue
the very nearby and far flung
as the population of the earth.
There's the promised land, but no Christmas tree.
He wants everything undone, Psalms unsung.
     *   *   *

Angel, in 50 years you'll be 105,
I might be celibate, more dead than alive.
When mountains are pebbles, I'll be 145.
Michael will have turned over a new leaf.
But it's still Angel, pudding and roast beef.
In Westminster roses will still bloom,
Trump is a poisonous mushroom.

I'll sing when I can't ride a stationary bicycle
I'll sing until my spit is an icicle.
     *   *   *

Everyday is somebody's birthday.
Light-years from now rhyme will not be over,
as long as there is gravity,
we can lean toward music,
we can jump with joy
and then come down.
This is not a poem, it's a shout:
HAPPY BIRTHDAY.
I could do this all day, the year is still a pup
until March 3rd, someday
in the year of our Lord I don't know.
The years are scrambled eggs
with bangers and bacon, no sweets,
until the earth is covered with ocean and fire.
Still as long as there is desire, the sublime,
death is here or there,
there will always be love somewhere
with a Mexican guitar, the reason for the universe.
La vida es un sueño,
when mankind tears up the calendar
life will be eternal as a urinal.

Truth or Consequences

1.

Today I'm alive in the Catskill Mountains.
I went to test my blood so I can avoid clots,
I crossed the Hudson, the Rhinecliff bridge.
I know it is written in the Quran
that man was "created from clots of blood."
Mohammed's great-great-great grandmother was Jewish.
I drove my automobile, a blue Odyssey,
with my dog Margie, named after my mother.
My mother would think it was sweet of me.
Margie plays games, retrieves my slippers,
chases groundhogs, deer, a fox.
She once caught a baby duck, spit it out alive.
She plays Truth or Consequences.

I know in New Mexico there's a town
named Truth or Consequences.
I'm far from Istanbul, but I jumped
off the Rhinecliff bridge, landed on the bridge
that crosses between Europe and Asia.
My father on sabbatical, we went to Turkey.
Shoes off, I explored the mosque
of Santa Sophia, I saw a miracle
I tried to understand. On Ancient streets
we bargained in English for hassocks and rugs
that I still have, not my fez that disappeared
when I went to war.
I will not bother you with ancient details:
nine years old, I was shot in my right leg
by a ricocheting bullet in Corfu,
in a celebration after a Greek revolution.

Back in the states, we drove to California.
We headed South: I saw chain gangs,

Jim Crow, 'Whites Only' churches.
African Americans, forbidden sidewalks,
diners, white bathrooms.
I knew nothing about the poll tax.

We crossed the continent at 45
miles per hour, stopped at Grand Canyon,
the Petrified Forest.
I can recall Reno, the Badwater Basin
260 feet below sea level,
lots of flat tires, dirt highways to Los Angeles.

A man, I flew, did not sail to Byzantium,
driving a Citroën Elysee, I found my way to Troy,
then to Ephesus and the Goddess Artemis.
I saw for the first and last time, the goddess
of the moon, the hunt, vegetation, and chastity
with her many breasts without nipples
that I see as bull's testicles.
I jumped up on a stage where she reigned.
With unwashed hands I touched her sacred front,
then her back few have seen:
half naked marble with a long delightful braid.
Thirty hands away on her sacred stage Aphrodite,
who has protected me all my life.
I met her for the first time,
I prayed in my New York City state Greek:
efcharistó, efcharistó, thank you, thank you.

Then a short walk away, I visited the Virgin Mary
and John the Baptist's graves.
There was a first, there is a second, perhaps a third coming.
Traveling and kisses have consequences.
Time and consequence are identical twins.
In my house there is a grandfather clock
of consequences, back to the wall, near a mirror

and books, time. I state a brave similarity:
if time is bread, every crumb, stale or fresh,
has consequences, especially if the bread
is the body of Christ.

2.

Translations have consequences. The time is Christmas.
O Tannenbaum, O Tannenbaum,
the carol loses truth for me when they sing
O Christmas tree, O Christmas tree.
I've heard "lug off the guts" translated in Italian
as "take away the tripe."
I don't know what crocodile tears are anymore.
Sunshine and rain have consequences,
still there are flowers that are night bloomers.
A consequence is a result, a lie is a falsehood.
There is the truth, no other word means truth.
A fact is not the truth. Hurray! I'm somewhere:
a metaphor may be the truth, a poem may be the truth.
I leap out of the standing room in the balcony
to the stage. I eat a sun and moon sandwich.
I'm all cheered up. The sun and moon may be bread,
clouds the ham and fromage. With Chianti
I prefer infidel sandwiches.
I refuse to eat God, that holy wafer.
That's the truth. I'll risk the consequences.

A Charming Story

Who is that creature in deep snow,
a question in the night,
on all fours, two knees and two gloved hands,
dragging behind two feet in grey woolen
socks? It was almost dark, 4 pm
in late December. I am that creature
dancing the deep snow waltz,
not the cakewalk, *The Make Believe
Ballroom* is forgotten.

I missed my luncheon, Today's Special:
snow and ice topped with pine needles
like chocolate sprinkles. What follows:
"my life shall have no dominion."

On my way to feed my donkeys carrots,
after half a mile in my blue Odyssey
the road was black ice, my wheels spinning.
I couldn't drive forward or in reverse.
Stepping out of the vehicle, I slipped
on ice. I caught onto my side-view mirror
that kept me from falling down hard.

No parachute, no "Mayday, Mayday,
S.O.S or Save Our Souls."
I chose to crawl on my hands and knees,
into darkness, I saw blood in the snow
a handshake before my head, neck and shoulders.

I couldn't tell if I was heading right
for the highway or straight to my backdoor.
I knew the trees I loved would lend me
a helping hand, a branch if they could. I thought
my trees know I don't want to freeze my sap.

That's common sense.
I am a 95-year-old child,
all the world's a stage of snow.
I have some teeth, one good right eye,
the left sees a page in sunlight, half in darkness.

I marched, left knee first, then the right,
my hands kept my face out of the snow.
I lived the pun: I had a running nose.

I remembered I asked physician friends
how long they thought I'd live.
In free translation they said,
"Half a cup of good years, if you don't fall down."

I reached three steps, my back door altar.
On my knees, I climbed the blue rocks.
I never heard of a God of snow or ice.
He is. He is a God without a face,
these days, the only God I believe in.

I am home, sitting shivering,
I am not sitting *shiva* for myself.
Ask your wandering neighbor what that means.
To Hebrews, sitting *shiva* is a wake.
Sitting shivering is a sacrilegious pun,
or perhaps I stumbled
on an eighth type of ambiguity.

I Don't Trust Alarm Clocks

1.

I see, look, observe, I clock,
stand watch with my thoughts
while my wristwatch is ticking.
Twelfth Night time pleases,
tickles me. Watches, like actors,
may tickle me or make me trickle tears
in a comedy, tragedy, or farce.
In sharp meter, syllabic or free verse,
a line will not scythe or beat me down.
In autumn I am not wheat or dry grass.
I watch out, time may tickle me to death.

I can laugh without stopping.
I was escorted out of the theater.
For saying "three tomorrows
creeping in their petty pace
are not enough." Half a second
and eternity are invisible, cruel.
I sound the alarm. Time is a lover.
There are many kinds of lovers, minutes, years:
time's a lover that fathers and mothers.
Make a child with time. Take care of your children.
Teach them music, to read and write. I suggest
the prelude and postlude to Corelli's *Pastorale*
and Bach's *The Sheep May Safely Graze*,
a final hymn, *Do Not Be Afraid.*

Time is a wonderful truth
that stops with a timeless kiss.
I write this posthumously
in the early morning of my life.

2.

I'm ashamed I spent the day writing
I Don't Trust Alarm Clocks, horrified
by an evil to the tenth power filthy soul.
Today there was insurrection, murder
in the capitol building: confederate flags,
lynch mobs, pro Auschwitz, anti gay,
anti women's rights, anti Latino, anti Muslim,
foaming at the mouth, anti trans,
anti Jesus motherfuckers,
served their United States of America.
I set my American flag at half mast
today and for ever, as Celan suggested.

I used to think I could change the world.
Now I know I can change my socks and underwear,
wash my face. I still think a poet
who writes a poem, whatever the shape of it,
makes the place where the poet sits,
the world a little better.

Long as a dog licks a wound,
a cat purrs, the planet is still young.
It's my dinner time, January the ninth,
2021. The date's my heavy date.
I call the world to dinner.
It's a different time now. Parsley eats bread.
All the names of the Bible are fasting.
I look, observe, watch the world.
Teeth are a better invention than the computer.
I'll keep time, I'll never, never trust an alarm clock.

Eye

While I ponder political uncertainty
while I hold on to my life raft
floating down the Potomac, the Seine, the Tiber,
simultaneously in a chapel, a kitchen temple
of confusion, a snail passes me by.
I want to get my way, have others do things my way.
I try to do things their way. Lady we will run away,
elope to a hideaway that's still hidden from us.
I tell myself what's new: another lady, Chloe,
her Greek Christian name, followed by
Garcia Roberts, wrote me half an hour ago.
She translates classical Chinese poetry.
I asked her to send me her poems.

Curiosity killed the cat and butterfly.
Saint Teresa of Avila was wary of curious novitiates,
but uncertainty makes my heart beat faster.
I run after the snail with my bound feet
in red slippers, wet from my dog's spit.
I ask the snail what's your name?
The same question Moses asked God.
I remember Moses was soon to marry
a dark skinned Nubian beauty. A snail
won't have 44 names like the God of Exodus.
The snail does not answer me,
waves its horns in sign language.
To the snail I am an evil giant. I pick up my rival,
a frightened eye in my hand retracts into
living darkness. I put him or her down on a safe path,
back in the race. How long does a snail live?
Will that snail outlive me?
Fish, grasshoppers, frogs are rivals of my watch,
not my sister. When I was six and she was ten,
I wrestled her gently, got on top of her,

pinned Lilly's arms to the rug-less floor
in Kew Gardens. It was the first war I won.
Years later Louise Nevelson remarked after I told her
I fought in World War II, "Yes and you won the war."

Now heart of hearts, I'm part snail.
I pass by myself, I try to be better than I am.
My voice and my soul pass my body, I say this:
I've stood on top of Mount Etna and Vesuvius,
in a nightmare I was a 6 feet 4 index finger,
my head was a fingernail. What was I good for,
born to pick the hot snot nose of volcanoes.
I believe a dream God dwells in his paradise
with sleep walking and dancing angels.
Lord, grant me sweet dreams. Am I sane, *meshuga?*
These days I often dream I am myself.
Yes my tongue was split in half,
I have more than a lot of broken bones
knitted together, scarred flesh
that may please a lady in my mind's eye.
An eye, I steal Leonardo's words:
who would believe that so small a space
could contain the images of all the universe?

Abortion

There is fantasy, invention, daydreams
metaphor, art and distant thoughts
within eyesight of one another.
A poet, a lady, wrote a poem recalling
an abortion she did not have,
perhaps out of sympathy, premeditation.
Later she married, had a much-loved son,
and three abortions. Her son fathered a child.
Whatever an abortion may be,
it refuses wonderful, unknowable possibilities.
To some it's murder and sin, whatever it is
it's not a walk in the country.

I shall consider: can a man have an abortion?
Is there a fetus within him, that he
could give birth to, pull out of himself?
Does he bury it, throw it in the garbage
or waste bin with food, not cans or newspapers?
If you start a poem with good lines
then cross them out, is that an abortion?
No, just ink, a pity, no blood, eyes closed,
no umbilical cord. Is a love affair broken up
for moral or financial reasons an abortion?
No, just a pity. So far if a man becomes a woman
he can't get pregnant. This poem is aborting now,
it's just an undeveloped metaphor, an image
that will not come out between my thighs.

Was my poet friend pro or anti conception? She certainly
doesn't believe in immaculate conception,
that Saint Anne was born without original sin.
It seems abortion gives birth to questions.

What I'm writing is a hunt, a shooting,
a fishing trip, nothing is shot, nothing is hooked.

Perhaps Failure has come to life bluntly.
I can nurse Failure, give him or her porridge,
meat, chicken when he or she has first teeth.
My Failure is the name of a new species,
I live in a metropolis of failures.
It's just like me to kiss my abortion goodbye,
possible child, never given a name,
for the hell of it, I'll call it Stan.

Zoopie

I bought an abused dog in Canada,
a golden retriever.
I renamed him Zeus, I kissed him.
After a day he fell off the dock
to the bottom of Lake Corry.
I dived down twenty feet, brought him up by the collar.
Eventually he learned to swim. The day he first swam
he barked to come into the house
after chasing squirrels and deer in the woods.
I kissed Zoopie, for God's luck.

A Scream

Since Covid-19, there's World War III,
a higher percentage of black than white casualties,
I scream my country 'tis of thee:
a masked face is not a motherly face,
naked faces may be death threats,
demand another Civil War.
Still, the Lord is a giver and taker.
The virus is a medieval 21st century golem,
he makes rivers of death flow down and upstream.
I've earned my right not to sing, I cough
I've earned my civil right to scream,
to love, to look. There is a fifth column, fascists
hiding, often policing round the world.

My memory is out of order, I remember
the French King gave Fleur-de-lis Catholic
money to pay for our Deist American Revolution.
Countrymen, the king went broke, caused starvation,
the French Revolution, lost his head.
I recall Kristallnacht, hundreds murdered,
November 9th, 1938, when Nazi's
broke synagogue and thousands of store windows:
the SS waltzing to the Horst-Wessel song.

Yesterday, our time, seditionists
attached by an umbilical cord to immortal hatred,
murdered on United States Capitol Hill.
I salute honest troops marching toward everywhere
in no-man's-land, empty streets,
a merry-go-round, Hiroshimas,
a World's Fair, roller coaster cars,
going up and down, around and around
with the unnecessary dead.

My Heart's Cousin

My tongue is gentle, my heart's cousin.
I am a family of one.
My eyes are my uncles, my ears my aunts,
mother is my mouth, father my penis.
I did not say he was a prick.
Because of my mouth and my penis,
I must honor myself.

I steal from my myself,
words, a poem, a pulled tooth with a gold filling.
Today it's 5:07 post meridian.
I must respect the time of Diana.
I can say anything I want to myself.
I say quickly: thanks to Frederick II,
Dante found terza rima in Sicily.
The king was excommunicated twice
by Pope Gregory IX.
I was excommunicated three times
by myself, once because I wrote, *Rope Stanley first.*
I did not say *Pope Stanley the first.*
I confess, I can only be forgiven
by myself. Sorry, Stanley.
You must discover what part of your body
your father is.

Numbers

I believe I understand why, others disagree,
Li Shangyin's poem: *Poem of Ten Lines*,
has nine lines. Li was showing, in his Tang way,
counting's never accurate. It's human nature to count.
"She has three children." Really?
One boy is half a man.
A good woman had three hundred and sixty five
painful days mourning her dead mother.
Hurrah for busy lovers
whatever their sexual persuasion!
They make love twice a day, every day of the year.
In this lunar year that is also a year of our Lord
there should be at least three calendars:
one for pain, one for joy, another timetable
for those who have orgasms because of missing trains,
nothing to do with Amtrak stations or airports.
I do not have necessary information
nailed to my kitchen wall. I refuse to count years.
I know during the tragic years
of mad Ireland's potato famine,
there was an abundance of Gaelic and English poetry,
in Dublin three kinds of potatoes were served
on every English restaurant table.

I look back at my confused years
and forward to a mirage of years.
Now, this minute, I'm not confused. I can see
something, someone who lived before I was born:
I have reason to love my grandfather Lewis
who died before my mother gave birth to me.
Why was I named Stanley, not Lewis?
She said, "I named your sister Lillian after him."
My mother, born in Philadelphia, only needed
one letter and she knew the word.

Perhaps I was named Stanley because
the Athenians lost the battle of Syracuse.
I'm thankful my parents, my uncles, aunts,
and cousins told me I should be grateful
to my grandfather. He crossed the Atlantic Ocean,
the Ocean that was an unexactly, unexactly,
unexactly place. My grandfather died
age fifty-five, of rheumatic fever
in nineteen hundred and twenty-four,
exactly one year before I was born.
My aunt Molly remembers the very day,
not that he used to swim across the Dudypta
to kiss my young grandmother.

Trick

You may trick a mother camel or goat
to feed on hay stuffed in the skin of her offspring
so she will give milk to serve her master
to an orphaned camel or kid.
In my tradition
one of the 44 names of God is breast.
I must find tricks to give the milk
of my love to the dead. I will
have to do more than show you my breast,
a fistful of my cut hair with the smell of me.

A Butterfly With Child

I discovered I was within a butterfly.
I wept for joy, my mother is a butterfly
flying to Mexico, inside of her and me
I flutter with anticipation:
soon I'll see sunlight and darkness.
I had a dream, I only dream the truth,
even when I was inside a chrysalis
I had come into my own,
although my mother cannot speak
English or Mexican. I have an intuition,
(I have more intuition than an elephant).
My mother was searching through the clouds
for her husband for more than a butterfly year.
He was chasing a young butterfly, another wife.
It came to me like lightning I've never seen.
When he found her, got close to her,
he saw she was a Christian moth
who when she alights, he tastes rabbits and mice.

We are Buddhists, Daoists, I will become
a patriotic butterfly. No, no, no, no.
My mother is a butterfly fighting
with a moth, who is more beautiful.
I've never seen the color red,
but blood red pollen covers me.
My mother miscarries. I am born.
I need a savior. I am a fly!
Not a hero or heroine.
I am anonymous. I pray to Buddha,
make me a firefly.

I, Stanley, have written two poems today
because the theaters are closed,
something like a play outside the play.

145

Carefully and carelessly I am caught
inside my own Mousetrap.
Wherever I was, I am an armed guard
fighting evil. Do not say I died,
place me among the fallen
with soldiers, sailors, and butterflies.

A Cup of Tea

How do you know you're getting older?
Boil water for a Hu-Kwa cup of tea,
go to your study, read and write a few minutes.
If an hour later you smell smoke,
the kettle out of water is blazing.
Do this twice a year, you're getting older.
You can buy a third kettle of the year
or you can boil water in a frying pan.
Why did they name that cookery a pan?
Proof the great God Pan is dead.

Reflections

There are incisions in the body of truth,
reality subject to surgery.
The truth has a useless appendix, a lie cut out.
I won't cut away visions poets saw and see.
A voice is a babbling tongue until a poet
makes you believe he or she saw that vision.
A devil generalizing has just spoken,
he's not the devil of death.
I ask specific angels, Michael, Gabriel,
to come to supper. They talk about sacred visions,
visits by Christ, the Virgin Mother, and Elijah.
On a hillside near Sienna, I've seen the Magi
on their way to to Jerusalem and Bethlehem
with a flute, cithara, and gifts.

There are schizophrenic visions,
the visionary may see herself or himself as anyone
who ever was. I have never seen myself
as anyone else, except when I am
represented in a dream in which
I don't carry an identity card.
I've never heard of any poet
who saw himself as a plate of spaghetti,
some of him wound around a fork
put in the mouth of a beautiful lady.

There are misreadings, wrong words read aloud,
the word *summer* seen as *some of her*.
I've misread words all my life. In the second grade,
I was marked down for misreading. I loved reading.
Bad grades for misreading knocked me down,
I got up, saved from knock out by reading poems.
Perhaps there is something profane in my misreading.
I want something, someone I don't know.
I did not know what I wanted.

At a launch in a London bookshop
I misread a word, I improved the poem.
Alas my imagination causes misreadings.
My one good eye sees something at a distance
and deep within me — a sight for my sore eyes.
In Long Island, walking toward the Montauk Highway,
I thought I saw a wounded swan runover
on Seven Ponds Road, trying to get up and fly.
When I was close to the white, struggling, not living thing,
I saw it was a white linen pillowcase,
half in a puddle on a tar road.
How did it get there, one hundred yards
from the nearest clothesline or pillow?
How far did the Atlantic ocean wind make it fly?

My vision was a fancy mistake that cut away the truth.
I am capricious, evanescent, that does not
mean I cannot tell good from evil.
Murder is evil, love is good. I don't murder.
An honest hangman and poet insists, "Each man kills
the thing he loves, needs a vulgar sometimes,"
I recite again a Spanish proverb,
"Do not talk of rope in a hangman's house."
When my lady totally ignores me, is it murder?
The child is rival to the husband.
I study husbandry, I obey a law opposite
primogeniture. Only ladies can inherit me.

Who else, what else might I be?
I consider that I am not human, I'm
carved out of a Redwood tree, I might be
a canoe. Anyone can paddle me westward
on the St. Lawrence river, paddle me near a waterfall,
against a wild current, toward a thousand islands,
not Niagara Falls. I could say it another away, still my way:
I am a crocodile eating reflections of fish.

Gods of Snow, It's Been Snowing All Day

It's a beautiful January day.
It's been snowing all day,
I've been reading beautiful books,
listening to beautiful music all day.
I'm snowed in. Beautiful snow on the roads
so deep cranky automobiles are blocked.
I don't know how to make a rejoicing snowman.
So much pleasure for part of today,
I denied death's existence.
There is Biblical snow. In parts of Africa
there was snow before there was light.

It's been snowing two beautiful days.
Notice the words on this page
are somewhat like snowflakes.
I put on my Deist snowshoes,
walk into the valley of snow,
past all the notices of private property,
into the snowstorms: trespassing
history, philosophy and geometry.
I find myself in ancient Greece.
I reach Delphi, I ask questions.
I find it is common knowledge
Chione is the goddess of snow, daughter of *Boreas*,
the North wind who abducted *Orithyia*,
child of the King of Athens.

Free Greeks, not the oracles, tell me
Chione is the mother of *Poseiden's* son.
With trepidation, I climb Parnassus,
I stop. It's night, I see an unknown moon.
I never reach the top peak of Parnassus.
The Gods do not see me, Chione is asleep.
She sleeps in a bed of ice with her dog
who looks like my golden retriever, Margie.

I slide down Parnassus on my ass,
all the way down, down to Aztec Mexico.
I get up with the help of a straw broom,
a symbol of work done by *Itztlacoliuhqui*,
the wintery death God who clears the way
for new life to emerge thereafter.

I know Gods are everywhere.
I bow and walk on.
Be certain, if I pray, I pray standing.
I am a hypocrite, respectfully
I walk and bow on and on.
I row on in my Catskill Mountain rowboat.
I reach the islands of Japan.
I dock then stand before *Okami*,
dragon and Shinto God of snow and rain.
Within his name in Japanese is
dark, darkness, closed.

Okami reached Japan from the South,
many centuries before the coming of Buddha.
Who are these Gods of destiny and snow?
In China the dragon brings good luck,
in Japan the snake often manifests itself
as a God of the sea, melted snow.
The Japanese sea Gods are often female water snakes.

It's almost dinnertime. I don't have time
to go to ancient Norway or Iceland.
By chance I land at Shannon.
I keen, weep without words,
because in my travels I have seen the world
on this beautiful day where the snow
is still falling. I go to dinner.
All my appointments are entrances
from stage right or stage left.

The Ferryman

I wanted to speak to the Ferryman.
I called directory inquiry, information,
on my smartphone. I was given a number,
a revelation. I swore to Hermes,
Gods' messenger, not to show or share
that sacred number with any human, king or serf.
I called, digital ladies' voices answered:
"He's busy." "Unavailable." "Occupied."

I remember the bloody and high voltage occasions
when the Ferryman was so close
I could smell and taste his breath.
After he came close to me
cat scans of my head showed I had an artifact,
a souvenir, a presence in an inoperable place,
camped under my hippocampus.

I've seen the Ferryman in paintings
and poetry, but never man's face to man's face.
Yes, I've known him all my life.
Death fathers everyone. I am his child.
Many in my neighborhood thought I was
an arrogant "black prince" and bugger.
Arrogant? I'm ashamed to tell the truth.
After World War II, I often wore black,
I limped like Richard III. Talk about the Styx,
my heart called for a horse, a horse.

I try to sing a hymn made out of holy facts.
Every sparrow knows Christ walked on water.
The Ferryman poled his ferry on dry land.
Dead drunk, I've seen him and his ferry in the sky
along the shoreline of Paradise.

Right now I see his ferry in the pond below my window,
the Ferryman in a rocking chair is bored with me.
He's waiting, yawning, smoking a cigar.
He blows clouds of smoke rings
across the lawn over a great red oak.
I call him respectfully. He won't speak to me.
Margie, my last dog, barks,
"Get the hell out of here!"
Does he ever ferry dogs, loving cats?
Rocking seems to entertain him.

I'm caught not saved, even though I praise
King David, Santa Teresa de Ávila
San Juan de la Cruz, the Ferryman who has
no name I know will eventually take me
by pole and his demon wings,
to an island where skeletons dance.
Now I think his accented Greek voice
is loud and clear. He's poling. He shouts my name,
I'm hiding. Clear across the Hudson Valley
I hear "Repent, repent." He's the double
of the statue of the murdered Commendatore
in Don Giovanni. I answer, "Your excellence,
Ferryman, statue, I invite you to dinner."
I've set the table with wine glasses,
New York State, Dutchess County red wine,
Hudson blue linen napkins,
knives, knives, knives, knives, no forks or spoons.
I know in a little while the Ferryman
will take me across the Styx in the company
of the four seasons, made human:
winter, spring, summer and autumn.
Summer wears a wreath of roses crowned with laurel,
Spring wears a waistcoat of budding dandelions,
Autumn, a coat of fallen maple leaves and grapevines,
wrinkled Winter has snowflakes in his hair and beard.
He wears ice snowshoes. I pretend to sleep.

I Don't Celebrate the Body Today

I don't celebrate the body today.
I want to celebrate guides of the soul to the afterlife,
to romp awhile with psychopomps.
They don't judge the deceased souls they guide.
I've seen them as birds gather in flocks
outside a house, waiting for someone to die.

In Christianity,
Saint Peter, the angel Michael and Jesus himself
lead the dead to Heaven.
Peter admits them through the gates.
For a thousand years
fleas, rats were sidekicks of the Reaper,
a skeleton with scythe, he led
half the world to the afterlife.

Soul music is Gospel with secular words. America
here is a parable: Jesus loves soul, Gospel,
jazz. He returns to Earth, he plays cornet and trumpet
in a jazz band outside an all-white church. Jesus
is lynched, not crucified. He sings Amazing Grace
with a rope around his neck.

Jews believe in arguments, sacred, secular.
They're occupied by the present, Torah,
and other holy, metaphoric books,
by their imaginations, profane and sublime.
Their magic is to make the unknown knowable.
They pay little heed to the waiting room, Gehenna.

Azrail is one of four angels
in the Muslim world. He is all seeing,
he keeps his eye on the Lote Tree of the End,
which grows in Paradise. When a person is born,

a new leaf appears on the tree with a name on it.
When it is time to die, the leaf falls,
which is Azrail's signal to come, to collect a soul.

Axmen, hangmen, those who work the guillotine and garrote
are babes in the wood.
I have no doubt
there are many nameless guides to the afterlife,
hundreds lit the inquisition fires.
With vulgar, sacrilegious haste, I send you
to the Ferryman, Charon, to Hindu, Buddhist
and Janist texts in Sanskrit. Confused,
I light a Chinese lantern: Mercury saved the Romans,
Aztec Xolotl, Black and white Heibai and Yuchang,
impermanence, two Chinese deities.
No God watching, Greek Hermes conducts
dead Myrrhine, priestess of Athena, to Hades.
I point a finger, broken by a Spalding baseball,
at Virgil guiding Dante.

There are some who believe that soul does not exist,
it's just a hole in the wall with a mouse trap
on the other side of the wall that catches nothing.
As far from Eden as I can get,
where the dove and the leopard wrestle,
I pass under the arch of Lorca's *Duende*. I adore
his poetry, plays, his soul, lovers and politics,
the gypsy girl frightened by the wind chasing her,
offered gin by the English counsel.
The rest is death and death alone.
Joyce, Yeats, Lorca, and Seamus in the balcony,
I refuse to play my Gilbert and Sullivan music.

Some guides confuse me.
Hannibal crossed the Alps on elephants.

The Japanese guide to the afterlife
is a name that describes a life.
God is dangerous to humans.
The Japanese Shinigami was a death with double suicides,
someone possessed by a God of death was selling paper.
The character who confronted death wrote "paper."

Joseph, the Virgin, and their infant
found their way to Egypt on a clear-eyed donkey.
The flight from Bethlehem to the Valley of the Kings,
500 miles of infants slaughtered behind them.

I'm writing a sinking ship's log,
not a catalog. I pity equally the sheep who leads
and the sheep who follow him or her to the slaughterhouse,
I write for the second time:
the Lord is my shepherd, I want, I want, I want.
It's round and round I go on death's merry-go-round,
looking forward and back. The Norse Valkyries are beautiful,
horseback riding battle virgins on a merry-go-round.
They collect dead warriors from the battlefield,
carry their dead to Valhalla where they continue
their favorite pastimes: fighting and feasting.

Some of the past is past among the Ancient Egyptians.
The god Anubis had a jackal's head.
He presided over mummifications. Eventually
Anubis led kings to the scales of judgement.
He weighed the heart against a feather. When the scales tipped,
in favor of the deceased they were granted
immortality, access to the afterlife.

Spirits traditionally wait at the foot of the deathbed.
A shaman accompanies souls of the dead,
helps birth, has another title: midwife to the dead.

Forever is a sorbet melting to *la nada*,
95 flavors, rainy days and nights wash away
until there are no storm clouds, no rainy days,
no sunny days, just centuries.
Centuries disappear like falling stars.
Something shrieks, a wolf, perhaps a newborn child,
a last laugh, a giggle, another laugh
then everything is over or under.

I follow poets most days and after conquests
through Saintsbury's *History of English Prosody*,
through castles, towers, and mud-huts.
They lead my body and soul through tradition.
I remember when I first studied arithmetic,
Auden saying to Cal Lowell,
"I'm afraid that poem was two poems, a mistake."
I remember the look on Auden's face
as if it were yesterday. He complimented Cal.
I could tell by his face, Wystan knew his place,
body and soul.

I Speak While Others Sleep

I speak while others sleep,
not in a classroom or theater.
I write my dreams down before I dream.
I dream that I am and I am not,
that is a good beginning.

I have evidence there is someone who
knows me well, I don't know at all.
I have arrogant and evil dreams.
I put a bit of soil in the crevice
of a granite boulder, a little dew, a little rain,
some sunshine, a miracle.
The rock abides. Now the rock holds a new life,
weeps when others weep, laughs,
but granite does not laugh
when people on crutches dance on it
or when a donkey is born who can't bray
or hee-haw. When the roads or paths are frozen
under deep snow, my donkeys want to see me.
I don't crawl now to feed them carrots
or apples, although I've crawled before.
It's petty of me, I pay a Mexican
to give them hay. I pay little attention
to those starving. No one makes soup
of boiling grass. It's something like cabbage.
It's a dream. I've written my dream down
before I dreamed it, the opposite: no ecstasy,
a little joy, no happiness in this speaking while others sleep

Today I Play Ring Around the Rosie

Because I've had a painful day,
can I get away with a poem that begins
with irrelevant arithmetic?
How many people have I seen alive?
Millions. I sat in a ten dollar seat
in Yankee Stadium on Memorial day
with 80,000 fans. I shouted "Olé!" with
aficionados in Seville and Madrid.
I've sung "God Save the King and Queen"
at the Old Vic. I'm fallible, naming English
theaters brings tears to my eyes.
Yes, I've been on crowded trains in China,
Times Square on a couple of New Year's Eves.
How many ladies and gentlemen have I seen naked?
I'm pleased to tell you charming lies,
Greek gods came to supper at my house.
They ate my pasta and fish soup with pleasure.
Pan asked for a recipe.
He said he loved my "dish", whatever it was.
It was spaghetti carbonara.
My heartbreak is my own business.

How many people have I seen dead?
Not as many as a gravedigger, but
I've seen a generous number with any part
of the body I can identify, gone. Why is it
that those who believe they're going to Heaven
don't die with more pleasure than dogs eat bones?
"Thou shalt honor thy father and mother."
Point of honor: I never saw my father dead.
I visited when he was in his final coma,
but I didn't want to look into his coffin.
I saw the soiled sheets torn off his deathbed.
I saw my mother dead, her traditional open mouth.

At least three women about to die, my mother,
my wife's mother, and another, threw off their blankets
lifted their nightgowns up to their necks.
A few days before she died, my mother said,
"I'm wounded." I told my mother,
"You showed me your wound yesterday."
She said, "I must have been crazy."

How many just borns have I seen
proudly held up in the air smacked
on the back for encouragement? Just two.
Why do I dial wrong numbers so often?
I can't help but hit a single number
two or three times instead of once
because my hands shake essentially.
I often shake hands with my strong grip.
How many fish and lambs have I eaten?
How many dying have I attended to?
A few. How many clouds have I adored?
Truth is, I don't know. Have I spent more time
in my automobiles than on sandy beaches?
You, who have also been kissed by a lake or river
(I don't care if you don't believe me),
the Atlantic loved me more than the Mediterranean.

By chance, in a notebook I opened,
I found that I had written a demand that endless
numbers of human beings insist upon —
for all I know, endless numbers
of creatures and trees: ecstasy,
I won't settle for joy or happiness.

Barbershop Conversation

This is barbershop conversation:
speakers have different histories,
different colors, palettes of thinking.
Working on a poem, painting with a brush,
calligraphy, is very different from saying,
"had a brush with the Red Guard in Beijing
in Red August." In the barbershop mirror, I saw
there were Aztec and hieroglyphic
painted words. In the old days, ladies
and gentlemen had servants comb
or brush their hair, indicating rank.
I have not forgotten wigs and snuff.

Whenever a word rhymes with a word, both
words have the other word as part of meanings,
however distant. Mark Twain wrote,
"History does not repeat itself, it rhymes."
Counting syllables and beats is more like
counting children than counting money.
With an endless need to brush up and shave
I want my poems to be news on the Rialto,
news of old and unanswered questions.
I work in a shop. You'll find me,
much of the time, beside a painted,
ancient red and white circling barber pole.
I offer leeches, surgery, conversation,
bleeding, I cut and brush beards.
The truth is not shampooed in my sinks.

The word "brush" is *Today's Special*.
I remember deer that ran into the brush,
to escape the hunter, I brush the stars,
my feathers brushed against the king's crown,
I never took the brush from a killed fox.
This is the way I speak in American.

I've cut myself shaving. I wanted to give
friends something to keep in their breast pocket,
a handkerchief, a fountain pen that's out of style.
Out of petrol, a French street cleaner
with a broom knows the difference between
a stylo and a plume. Before the waltz,
Frederick Barbarossa was coronated,
he had a red beard. When I was a child,
they played *Largo al Factotum* from *Il Barbiere*
to stop me from crying. Then they laughed.

I Praise Scientists

I praise scientists who have stuck tiny waterproof
microphones, womb deep. Fetuses can't
make out a mother's words inside her womb.
Fetuses can hear prosody, inflections, accents
a pause, the rising and dips in a sentence.
We exit the womb with a scaffolding of language
well in place. French two-day-olds cry, wail
on a rising pitch contour, mirroring
the melodic patterns of spoken French.

A Fable: Christ's Eagle Fathered Eagles

In Granada, I heard a basso sing
while an altar boy played a blue guitar
that belonged to a wandering half Jewish,
half Gypsy girl. Rita cried out an offer
to Christ's Eagle: if he alighted
on her bare forearm (she knew her arm would bleed),
she would give the raptor a manicure,
and scratch its back. It was common knowledge
her father drank *Anis de Chinchón*, a blood thinner
so he would not get a blood clot that might
blow out the candlelight,
switch off the electric light in his brain.
It was five o' clock in the afternoon of my life.
Gypsy Christ changed from Jew lily to Spanish sunflower.
Most women dressed in black, mourned five years
when a benighted family member died.
For many gentlemen, it was customary:
mass Sunday morning, bullfights at five o'clock,
a house of whores at night.

A Dominican friar who had a dog
with a flaming candle in his mouth,
told everyone who would listen, "Everything,
with a heart bleeds a little of Christ's blood —
thanks to the poor who give to others much
that they receive in charity.

I hear silence:
some are praying, no one is singing.
From a lectern with a carved Eagle,
I speak to the congregation.
Rivers and oceans have no blood,
anybody floating who speaks or sings
with an open mouth, a person

who has bleeding gums, bleeds Christ's blood.
Human teeth are made of the same ivory
as elephant tusks, they do not bleed.
It follows whoever, perhaps an angel,
invented blood, invented the heart,
the first heartbeat, the first little bang.
Why did Jesus choose to visit the world?
He invented pebbles, wouldn't that
have been enough? A child interrupted,
"Before there were pebbles there had to be rock."
Another lad shouted,
"There was light, water, and urine."

I explain in a louder voice, so those
washing their hands in holy water, can hear:
First there was nothing. Nothing comes of nothing.
If you want to contradict me, leave the room,
keep to your house of worship, or turn on your tv.
There were innumerable storms,
weather without elements
clouds without intelligence,
disagreements, arguments,
before there were laws,
before there were words, principles, evidence,
long before creation there was self evidence.

Thomas Jefferson wrote in a letter,
"United we fall, divided we stand."
Among Ancient Greeks, Eros was an explorer.
He had misadventures. What cities could he construct
with a broken wing? Still, Eros wanted love and sex.
He made the sexes one by one, then two by two.

Brothers and sisters,
the universe is an umbrella. I see more umbrellas
than at Jones Beach, Lido, Shanghai, Dover Beach.

Because it's raining galaxies, dark holes, quarks,
protons, I crawl under the periodic table,
I look under the skirt of physics, between her legs.
Flights of light years are operatic.
I translate what I hear, remember my purpose
is to write a poem, personal pronouns and adjectives
are falling stars — stars are cow dung in the pasture
that is the firmament.

I've been scratching the back of Christ's Eagle.
The Eagle just brought me a gift
of a deer mouse. To show affection
the Eagle puts its head in my neck.
I try to kiss the Eagle on the mouth.
Christ's Eagle flies away from me.
To kiss an Eagle on the mouth was my folly.
Never for a moment in my life did I think
my follies did not make sense. I add
for good luck, I know in France,
une folie is also a mansion of pleasure.

Once I thought I was an individual.
I look out from my farmhouse window,
I see part of me is that and that and that,
those and those and those.

Ode to Opposites

1

Every day I'm getting younger, not older.
I like talking in opposites.
It doesn't really make a difference now
if the compass in my head points south or north.
I grow on the north side of a tree.
Lovers, my *no* may mean *yes*. My good eye
helplessly shows what I love. I fight
to kill everlasting death mano a mano
but I want to lie alone in my grave
with the ashes of my dogs at my feet,
the ashes of thirty two paws at my feet.
I'm getting younger not older,
my mind has changed
except about good and bad.
I believe in opposites. The opposite of chance,
the uncertainty of good soup, borscht and minestrone.
Bread and wine are transubstantial possibilities.
I sometimes spit out certainty.
I'm writing this as proof I'm getting younger.
My poetry can jump rope with your dog or cat
for a long life. I tell you I knew Walt Melon,
I didn't say watermelon.
He swam backstrokes from old lakes to old rivers.
One afternoon Walter fell off a waterfall.
In these words there's a sliver of poetry,
crows exist by eating my run over, dead words.

2

Young, I desecrate a Psalm.
I'm old enough to vote.
I'll turn right side up for fresh air.
I do not love my neighbor who wants polling stations
fifty miles from where black folks live,

get them off white sidewalks,
imprison them with the insane, the sick,
throw away the key. I spend useful time
looking for the key to unlock prisons.

My soul is jailed by my body,
chained to a nest of iron bars,
fires melted together.
I live in an iron basket
filled with the fruits of my labor.
I don't eat fruit except blueberry pie.
My three donkeys are believers,
I have an agnostic horse, a farm full of massacres,
born, reborn and unborn wildlife,
silent and multilingual trees, flying snakes,
humming birds whose wings beat a hundred times
a second on my watch that stopped long ago.
I feed and I'm fed upon by
the unlisted passengers on Noah's Ark,
they travel steerage as my ancestors and I did.
Eros is a stowaway on the Ark.

Ares, god of war, and Eirene, goddess of peace,
despise their faint hearted armies.
Aphrodite, dancing on water, follows us
with her ways of making mainsails and jibs
proud to be what they are. I had the fortune,
to swim with half naked Aphrodite all my life
in the Hudson, Meander, the Tiber, the Sligo,
in the rapids and monosyllabic creeks
that dry up in hot summers, but are always water again
when the ice breaks up in the spring.
Whatever the weather, I'm growing younger, not older.
I was born on June 21st,
the first day of winter in Australia down under.

Spring 2021

An American Corinthian Column
supports the roof of my house,
where swallows nested ten years.
They came last spring despite twenty inches of snow.
They're not here this spring. It's a kind April day.

I wish I knew how to call my swallows.
They are privates like me,
my buddies, male and female
in a war against ugliness and evil.
They may have fallen.

It's a foolish April day. My swallows
were never interested in conversations
on my porch under their nest. I protected
their eggs in the nest from racoons, snakes and eagles.
They made me feel safe, not lonely,
despite my lover, close friends, music and books.

Did my swallows die when a great Polish poet died?
I don't think they've gone to Poland to build their nest.

Father swallows are heroes. If the proud sitting
mother and nest of eggs are attacked by a raptor
the handsome male bird swoops, dives down then up,
leads eagles away. If our father swallow survives
he brings horseflies, worms to the nest.
Lonely chaos, my mind is scattered. Desperate,
I throw sacks of mixed seeds that grow tall
in the fields where my happy donkeys graze.

* * *

I cannot make a swallow's nest. I bought
a bat house I tied to an oak tree's crotch.
I search the sky. The poor ones who live highest
on earth are jumping spiders with eight eyes.

167

They live in ice atop Mount Everest.
Come what may or June,
I am ready to throw away this discourse.
I need some days not to write anything
but letters, sign checks, and protests.
I have found a Chinese bronze horse
with one foot poised on a flying swallow.

I'm up most of the night, listening for swallows,
I hear Canada geese innuendo.
I follow sparrow politics. *Compañeros*,
I'm for giving every living thing a vote,
the just born and dead the vote.
                              The dead
are patriotic. They've got death, they want liberty.
They fly a flag, an unwrapped shroud
or prayer shawl half mast on a flag pole.
Holy rivers get ashes and flowers, most Chinese
mourn their dead, foreheads on earth. I pity
those who choose to be entombed with unfortunate
live dogs, a pipe and tobacco. Enough.

If I had to choose what day I wanted to be born
I'd choose the first day of summer.
The farthest One gave me my wish.
This winter, I was snowed in by ice. One night
I dreamed I stood beside a six-foot dandelion.
I've shrunk. Now I'm only two inches taller
than the dandelion. The kind sun wakes me
wishes me good morning. The first dandelion
of spring appears on my lawn.
In a dandelion world, I ache for swallows.

Swallows, citizens, dreamers, have our evil
politicians and climate change murdered you?
I chatter, I'm lost and frightened.
Who am I to teach swallows I don't feed?

Poetry is not a secret voting booth, an absentee ballot.
Prose is opinionated. In my other early life,
I voted for cuneiform, hieroglyphics,
Nahuatl in Mexico.
I'll vote, sing again in a band.
To sing the blues is patriotic.
Today is election day. Today is today.
Tomorrow is a world away.
Humans look like the farthest One and alike.
I have some resemblance to a male evergreen.
Everything in the world rejoices,
everything is left with a broken heart.
There are stars on Earth, but I'm informed
by what is light years away, and by ants
that found their way into my desk drawers.
I hunt beauty. I accept the gift.
I once wrote, "I must make my death handsome."
I have hands and fingers, like wings, feathers.

I have a knapped heart and a calling,
my outspoken interruptions are something
like a weathervane on the roof of my house.
Of course I'm out of style, I'm north
south, east, and west.
In a canoe in Canada, I was blown around
and around by a tornado, a 200
mile per hour wind that blackened the sun
on a July afternoon.
I would prefer to be knocked over
by the wind of a passing butterfly.
Today I believe
I would never welcome that butterfly.
I sign my letters *faithfully, much love,*
not *sincerely* or *yours truly*, or *my best.*
I would consider, *Yours still standing, once rooted,*
Stanley

*See *Swallow* poem, page 90

Little Song

There are little songs, syllables counted, rhymed,
disappointing loveless sonnets. Look,
look at our bodies we are made to love and work.
There is loveless work, there is no loveless love.
There are Lordly oceans not crossed
or loved by everyone.
Creeks and rivers flood   dry up.
Rivers may experience an undressing,
an *expolio,* a crucifixion,
a transubstantiation.
There are lovable floods.
Rivers may become Lordly.
The Nile, the Mississippi have alluvial deltas.
There are delta sonnets full of mud, gravel and love.

Year

What are years? In early Chinese waters
there was a monster named Year, she came
to harass womankind and mankind at a fixed date
at the beginning of Spring. Later a wise man
taught people to explode fireworks to scare
the monster away. It became the custom
to explode fireworks on New Year's Day.
Now there is a frightened monster, nothing like
a dragon that brings good luck to the worthy.
I don't have words to say what Year looks like.
Yes, Year has eyes of many colors, donkey ears
for music, webbed warrior feet, an anus
for disapproved holidays.
Year holds public property that is not hers.

In short, to the God fearing, Year looks like history,
has several deceiving eyes. Still, for a month's sake,
Year modestly hides in the forest and in kind waters.
All years are rare. A few of us believe
Year has children. I think there is a continuing.

Born in Winter, there are premature years.
Forest fires are incubators.
There are so many wildfires in California,
Mother Year and Father Year often made love
under sequoias. It's a long swim for Year
from San Francisco Bay to Shanghai.
Year rests in Hawaii. Twenty summers ago,
Year swam in the Grand Canal to the Biennale,
her tail splashing laughter at the biannual
that had nothing to do with Year.
What did opinionated paintings, painted for beauty
and money, have to do with the monster?
No one painted mortality, eternity for nothing.

A happy few saw Year on Loch Lomond's bonnie banks.
An Irishman near the Sligo told me in a pub
he saw Year fighting with a minute,
and minute won. Dead drunk, I told him
when I swim in the Hudson River,
backstroke, freestyle, and kicking
with my one good leg, sooner or later
I know Year will devour me. Till then,
I molest Year in Januarys, try to capture her.

Year understands languages. All languages,
including Chinese, have ancient African roots.
There are 46 Aboriginal dialects in Mexico alone.
Year survived the 1520 genocide in Mexico.
Year after year, she is amused
at the toast in Polish, "A hundred years."

Year struggles, aristocratic Time says
"Year has a Cockney accent."
The loneliest fisherman in the world,
I try to spearfish an extra Year for me,
as if it were a whale.
There are years of many colors,
black, white, purple, green years.
I don't forget a year that looked like a sparrow,
flew like an eagle. She flies forever like some
waterbirds, never touching water.
Year is a clean word, a bullet shot
in the temple of the head.
Forever and *always* are dirty words.
"Words have no word for words that are not true."

Year holds open his or her mouth,
fills it with ocean and spits Time in my face.
Year spits salty wrinkles on my face.
I don't lie, I write on the way to Truth so you

believe what I say. Year isn't a metaphor,
a Bible story. I laugh and say, "Leap year is not
an extra day in February, or a leap over
a tennis net of days." I don't want to waste words.
I kiss Year the monster with her many tongues,
I make good use of my tongue that is guilty and innocent.

Preface II

Now Preface is not fired or homeless,
but it is a poem looking for a job.
I let Preface sleep in a spare room.
It walks in its sleep, mumbles,
Once I was necessary, now I'm like
an old prayer preface put in a Western
wall crevice. But I'm not a prayer,
I'm an old bearded, grey-haired preface
looking for work. I found it. I'm not an echo,
I refuse to close the door of a book.
My refusal to close a poem is another
proof, I'll die refusing to die. I don't
believe it, but I'll say "Death is a preface."
I will not change the title of my old Preface.
Carve Preface on my gravestone.
I consider a preface is just a little foreplay.

Fact Song

I don't walk the streets with a sign: Poetry Not for Sale.
Why, how, did I do the harm I've done?
I've eaten whale meat in Barcelona.
The worst thing I ever did
was something I should have done:
I never told my mother she had a bastard
grandson. I was trembling and afraid
my always angry father, "God's angry man,"
would blow his stack at me.
It would be hard for my mother to see
the son she loved ever again except in secret.
When my mother was cremated, I planted her ashes
under her favorite flowers, Montauk daisies,
father was at a home for senior citizens.
He needed around the clock nursing.

I introduced my son to father and sister.
Father told my sister to see that my son
got a full grandchild's share in his will.
My sister, with her husband,
who "moved the arsenal to the atomic age,"
he miniaturized the atom bomb,
(worked with Wernher von Braun after Hiroshima).
All our rockets are still pushed up by
what he thought and did.
My heroic brother-in-law and sister
were my father's executors.
My sister disobeyed. My son got nothing.
My share was the same as a grandchild.
In my mother's album of family photos,
I appear on page 13. Reader, I wrote
some useless words, some of this before.
Now I've twisted, not a meal, a merienda I cooked
on a wood and would not stove.
I'm 95 years old plus ten difficult months.

If Someone Makes Love Anywhere on Earth

1.
Hatred begets climate change.
Hatred is proud and microscopic,
hatred has a tailpipe of smoke,
coal fires, gas burning evil air.
Iago and Esso sound alike,
put money in thy purse.
If someone makes love anywhere on earth,
love is like climate change,
lovemaking in China cleans the air
in London, Los Angeles, and Beijing.
A great wall of solar libido
protects us from barbarian hatred.

Such circumstance is not a butterfly effect.
Love carries grief on his or her shoulders,
as if grief were a child. Grief is a foundling,
love sometimes is a birth father or mother.
"The present is pregnant with the future."

In time, the oceans will dry up,
the deserts will become oceans.
Please become a lover, sooner the better.
I hear idle readers say, "There he goes again.
He thinks the dead are dancing skeletons."

Yes, I think every maggot is a detective.
There is an honorable thing to do:
be a thief, steal beauty, spend it,
give it to the poor, to any passer by.
Hot news: if music is the food of love, play on.
If I live long enough, I'll have a bookship
that sails around the world, unloading my cargo.
If I were the north wind, or just a breeze, I'd blow
Johann Sebastian Bach notes to Asia.

2.

I write, it is the 6th of May,
summer is just around the corner.
This year is next year.
Clouds or cloudless days predict the future.
I'm something like a cloud flying by.
Life and death, love and hate are clouds flying by.
I'm a cloud who can't stop wishing. I'm spinning.
I know that scientists proved time is made
of nanoparticles that rotate beyond
three-hundred billion revolutions per minute.

3.

I'm sitting at my desk with my feet on a chair.
Rights and wrongs differ from country to country,
street to street. Sooner or later
gravity may become unconstitutional.
Of course there are many nameless places
in the universe without gravity, silence perhaps,
with unpredictable election lights.

What I write is informed, is a freight train,
cattle cars once occupied by Jews, homosexuals,
do gooders, gypsies on their way to death camps,
slaves escaping on the underground railroad
north to Canada, south to Mexico.
Even my love poems are informed
by what I just said. For truth's sake,
I'll change the climate of this poem.
Here is a chilling, dangling, political metaphor:
when in 1938, Byron's tomb
was opened for examination,
his right foot had been cut off,
lay at the bottom of the coffin.
The world is getting colder and warmer,
countries will drown, books will swim.

Detour

For God and country's sake,
I'll sink the ship *Not Yet*.
I pretend to carry some truth in the hold.
The truth is sweet un-American: rather than
Pennsylvania Hershey bars, I prefer
churros con chocolate in Madrid,
gnocchi to Idaho potatoes.
Confusion, Confucius, what's the difference?
I've got the hots for Homer snoring
in the pines. My favorite saints are
Christopher, who no longer is a saint,
Julian, who murdered his mother and father.
I prefer rhyming transubstantiation,
not with the stations of the cross,
but with Washington D.C. Union Station,
where I sat down and wept.

I believe in my own preoccupations,
Gods and dogs.
I've spent more time in Catholic churches
than synagogues.
I have no memory of ever wetting the bed
until I was ninety. Often I don't recognize
names I know and lines I know by heart,
or my face in a mirror. I'd rather walk
into the British Museum, the Prado
than a Museum of Modern Art.
But I cut high school when I was thirteen
to see Matisse, Modigliani, Pollock,
Picasso's Guernica on 53rd Street,
Russian movies. I met ladies
who mixed up their love of art and me.
I read Lorca, Rimbaud, Valéry and Hart Crane
before Whitman. I enjoy telling my history:

age nine I was shot in my left leg
by a ricocheted bullet in a celebration
after a Greek revolution. Until I was four or five
I thought World War I was just a fairytale.
At six I knew about babies killed in bombings,
dogs fighting over delicious baby legs.

I never took a class in art history,
I was taught by museums, artists,
Zeri, K. Clark, Milicua, who liked to
eat with me, my free verse conversation,
my unaccountable eyes for quality.
Life was mostly pleasure, I didn't like pop art,
for surrealist fun I painted punctuation,
multicolored question marks, sexy nuns.
French artists know how to remember ladies.
If I ever teach gallantry at the Courtauld,
I'd teach the world's students to paint
their own experience, what was
Courbet's *Origin of the World*,
their naked woman they see in bed
neck down to beautiful thighs above her knees.

If I teach the Psalms, I'll give
special attention to Psalm 38,
King David's misbehaving.
If *Not Yet* isn't a sinking ship
it's not a highway, it's a single lane
with someone holding a sign:
STOP then GO SLOW,
or a road completely blocked with a sign,
an arrow to the left that says DETOUR.

The grounded ship *Not Yet* sinks.
My body swims ashore,
a guest who knows the hospitality

of beaches and sunlight.
My soul swims out to sea,
towards Tsunamis and doldrums,
a host of ocean waves.
What's the difference?
The Gods murder all their guests.
I kissed Margie goodbye dead, her eyes wide open.
Next morning, she looked peaceful,
I kissed her right front paw.

Haiku

Margie died,
my pubic hair fell out,
I'm covered with lice.
It's worse than that.

A Little Afternoon Music

In cement playgrounds there are
8-year-olds who will be mothers and fathers,
grandmothers and grandfathers
(years equal to six, seven or eight dog lives).
I see grandmothers and grandfathers in swings
and slides, some jumping rope.
In a tree playhouse, three canes, candy,
crutches, walkers with wheels and brakes.

This year's violets outside the playground fence
have come again. They are religious.
Without vanity, a congregation of wildflowers
bloom and are blown away
from baptism to last rites,
from circumcision to Kaddish.

The 8-year-olds in the schoolyard

play catch with balls, images of the globe.
Soon, they shout with a mouth of pulled teeth
they have swallowed one by one,
with blood of bleeding gums, their *Beaujolais*.

Opera pleased my dog, she smiled at my Zoroastro.
For her I played on a washboard a little afternoon music.
She liked that, she jumped in my lap, licked my mouth.
For Margie I scrubbed and scrubbed notes
Until my knuckles bled.

This is a little afternoon bleeding music.
There are so many poems on the deaths of animals.
Margie died three days ago.
I've nothing to do but write this, out-of-key growl,
at a cruel, disobedient God and my good dog
who liked me to growl at her, one of our games.
My dog sat, came to me when I called her.
Holy, Holy, Holy, dog amen.

No God comes to sit at my table at my invitation –
call it prayer.
God doesn't smile when I scrub hymns on a washboard –
my knuckles bleed.
I know differences between dogs and humans.
Holy, Holy, Holy, dog amen.

the great god IS

Holy, holy, holy without a God.
Was ist, won't be,
there is life expectancy,
there are subjects, citizens
of a nest, a flower,
cared for, attended by a gardener.
There is no King in a garden.
I'm offended by the Lord, "King" in the Bible.
The Nile is not the King of rivers.
The Rose of Sharon appears
in the Song of Songs and in my garden
where sunlight and rain are words of the Preacher.
What rank is a hurricane,
not Pope or Dalai Lama.

When they curse each other forever,
Arab and Israeli, do it in the other's language.
There is the god IS.
I don't know who sits
at the right hand of IS.
Was ist, IS, isn't a communist,
capitalist, socialist, or anarchist.
IS kissed me. There IS design.
IS created the universe.
I said "No thanks," yesterday to IS.

I plant my vote for trillium for any office,
waterlilies are my constituents.
Was ist? I vote for a flower,
FREEDOM,
I wear that flower in my hair
in or out of bed.
The winds are not anarchists,
there is an anarchist in me,

I'm King of the Chair
I sit in this morning.
My subjects are books.
I'm also a commoner.
I'm an unnamed character in a book,
a passerby, a pronoun.

I am not what I eat.
I am not a man of my table cloth.
Really? I dine on myself.
I still eat a poem of myself.
Now I'm my dog who finishes
my oatmeal in the morning.
Yes, I bark at myself,
"do some good."
IS is not my shepherd.
I am God forsaken,
I praise IS, the maple tree nearest me.
I am saved by trees that give me breath.

If I get what I'm writing
into a construction I have a religion.
I have a religion,
belief that is holy.
Holy, holy, holy without a God.
These are the last lines I write,
I make them first.
"In my end is my beginning."
Holy, holy, holy without a God.

Afterword

Fu Hao

I became acquainted with Stanley Moss through the late Israeli poet Yehuda Amichai. It was around the beginning of 1991 when Yehuda learned that I was translating his poems and asked a publisher friend of his in New York to send me some books of his poetry. The publisher was Moss. He sent me two copies of Amichai's poetry published by his Sheep Meadow Press, along with a copy of his own book of poems, *The Intelligence of Clouds* (1989). From then on, we began a correspondence and friendship.

From March to September 1993, I was visiting the University of Cambridge as a British Academy K. C. Wong fellow. One day, Moss wrote to me saying that he had arrived in London and asked me to meet him at the hotel where he was staying. I went and found there a sixty-five-year-old smiling gentleman, tall and grey. It was morning. He looked as if he had just got up, in an amiable mood. Having exchanged pleasantries, he called for brunch, and we ate and talked in his room. After the meal, he took out the copy of my poems in manuscript I had sent him previously for his advice, and we began to discuss and revise them one by one in great detail. After revising a dozen or so pieces in a row, he said he was tired and wanted to rest, so I left. It was past noon.

Later, I translated some of Moss's poems and published five of them in a Chinese magazine *Poetry Monthly*, No. 6, 1995, two of which were about China, and in 2003, my compilation and translation of *An Anthology of Twentieth Century Poetry in English* came out, including four of them. On a previous occasion, he sent me a fax saying that a foundation was going to give him a grant to publish a book of poems translated into a foreign language abroad. He preferred Chinese and asked me if I would undertake the translation, and, as the grant had a deadline, asked me to reply as soon as possible. Unfortunately, for various reasons, I could not accept the offer in time.

During 2005-06 when I was visiting UNC at Chapel Hill as a Fulbright scholar, Moss called repeatedly, inviting me to stay for some time at his place in New York. In late June 2006, I was invited by the East Asia

Department of Wesleyan University in Connecticut to give a reading on the recommendation of another friend, the sinologist Professor Vera Schwarcz, so I decided to stop by New York for a week before we headed far northeast. When I arrived in New York with my wife and son by train, it was already past ten o'clock in the evening, and Moss himself met us at the Grand Central Station. As soon as we entered the door of his house in the Bronx, he told his Philippine maid to serve the chicken noodle soup prepared beforehand by himself and watched us eat it before we went to bed. During our stay at his home, Moss revised more of my poems and said they were "very bad", which I understood as referring mainly to my English, and I was not quite convinced at that time. Now I come to realize that he was right, for men improve with the years, as W. B. Yeats said, and I, with my English improved more or less, can see clearly by myself what was wrong with my past writing. He also showed me how to write impromptu by asking me a series of embarrassing personal questions and writing down my answers. I have told the story in detail in my book *Secrets: How I Write Poetry* (2011). He also gave me some of his newly published collections of poems and other poets' books published by his nonprofit poetry press, indicating his willingness to cooperate in the future.

After I returned to China, I was busy with academic research and writing, and the publishing situation of serious works in the country was getting worse and worse, so I was able to do nothing but have translated two more poems of Moss and published them in *Poetry Monthly*, No. 8, 2008, as an account of my commitment at that time. It was not until May 2014, after he had received a copy of my English translation of the famous Chinese poet Xu Zhi-mo's works published in China, that he expressed clearly his intention to publish in China a book of his own poems in Chinese translation. Considering his deep affection for China, I felt obliged to help him fulfill this long-cherished wish. After contacting several official publishers and being rejected, I thought of Mr. Chu Chen, a freelance publisher who had published several books of mine before. Thanks to Chu Chen's promise and earnestness to collaborate, I dared to start selecting and translating then. Mainly from the two recent books of poetry that Moss had sent me, *God Breaketh Not All Men's Hearts Alike* (2011), a selection of his best pieces from various periods, many of them in revised and final form, and *No Tear Is Commonplace* (2013), I translated 148 poems and a piece of prose memoir.

According to his own account in his memoir, "Diary of a Satyr", and correspondence with me, Moss began to write poetry at first under the influence of William Shakespeare, William Blake, Arthur Rimbaud, Garcia Lorca, Wallace Stevens, W. B. Yeats, James Joyce, Paul Valéry and Hart Crane. That showed that from the very beginning, the influences he received were international and transcultural. Later he made friends with many poets of different cultural backgrounds, including W. H. Auden, Stanley Kunitz, Theodore Roethke, Dylan Thomas, W. S. Merwin and Yehuda Amichai, and was more directly influenced by them. Therefore, his poetry contains both the distinct flavor of American localness and the exotic colors of multiculturalness; it does not belong to any school of modern poetry, but has various traditional elements. A large part of his concern is with daily life, involving personal experiences of his own and of the people around him, and family, friendship and even emotional connection with pets are recurrent themes in his poetry. In that sense, his writing is somewhat   similar to traditional Chinese poetry. Some Western scholars have criticized traditional Chinese poetry for being trivial and banal, not metaphysical or transcendental enough, but it is actually the quality closest to the essence of poetry, that is, humanity. Poetry should not only be something remote and beautiful, out of imagination and f ictionalization, but also be something warm and touchable, out of real feelings. It is such kind of strain that I admire most in Moss's poetry, together with necessary narrative details.

As a child, Moss traveled with his parents to many places in Europe, Asia, and Africa along the Mediterranean coast, and was deeply impressed by different cultures as well as landscapes. His poetry is characterized by a wide range of subjects and materials from exotic cultures and histories, though his vision of the world is always that of an urban American. His writings, like his travels, have explored keenly many places in history and in reality, sketchy in their perceptions, but honest in their attitudes. Most noteworthy are his writings on Chinese and Jewish subjects. Like many Jews, Moss seemed to have a natural liking and curiosity for all things Chinese. His works show his great affection for his Chinese friends ("Letter to Alexander Fu, Seven Years Old", "To Angelina, Alexander's Cousin, Whose Chinese Name Means Happiness"), his keen interest in Chinese culture ("China Sonnet", "April, Beijing", "On Trying to Remember Two Chinese Poems", "China Song"), and even his lovely showing-off of

Chinese knowledge ("The Hawk, the Serpents and the Cloud", "The Grammarian", "Peace"). He taught in Beijing in 1987 and on the cover of his book, *The Intelligence of Clouds*, he repeats what a student from Peking University said, and the class agreed, "Of all the foreign poets who have read to us, Stanley Moss's poetry is the most Chinese."

Although born into a Jewish family, Moss was brought up an atheist who believes only in "No God" ("Song of No God") and continued to be a pragmatist who prefers to worship the Egyptian animal gods ("In the Rain"). He believes that life is sacred, including snakes. He is not a Buddhist, but W. S. Merwin, poet and Buddhist, once said to him, "Stanley, you're a better Buddhist than I am." He values wisdom passed down orally from generation to generation by family members more than religious doctrines ("Godmothers", "Scroll"). In addition, perhaps related to his personal preferences or his profession, he has shown a good knowledge of traditional Western literature and art, and seems to have a particular fondness for classical mythology. "A History of Color" is an intellectual masterpiece, akin to John Keats's "Ode to a Grecian Urn", but richer in content and with a unique point of view. He also likes to use "characters" in classical myths as metaphors, taking the satyr as his own personality and the centaur as his father's, and skillfully rendering and highlighting the character traits and privacy of their respective lives, which are otherwise difficult to describe straightforwardly ("Satyr Songs", "A Satyr's Complaint", "Centaur Song").

Forest Gander recently wrote about Stanley Moss's poetry, "in our epoch of turmoil, crisis, grief, I find that Moss's poetry still, always, brings be a little closer to happiness." Indeed, rare is valuable, as we Chinese say. Perhaps he will meet more of his understanding friends in China. After my translation of his *Selected Poems* was published in China in 2015, there have been many positive comments from Chinese readers on the Web. Here I quote and translate a few of them as follows:

"It's like a voice that I have been searching for years."

"Not many of Moss's poems are to my taste in their entirety, but often a line or two in his portrayal of everyday things can open one's mind to write a completely unrelated poem."

"Sometimes powerful, sometimes gentle, everywhere glowing with whimsy, if there is one word to describe it, it is *marvelous*; there is no genie, but everywhere a stone is turned into gold. He said that Chinese people paste spring couplets above the lintels of their houses and enter and depart through the doors of poetry every day. Why didn't I think of that? Sometimes poetry exists as the collective unconscious."

This time, Moss has put together a thematic book, including as the main part poems about China and influenced by Chinese philosophy, history and experiences, saying that he realizes how much China, Chinese poetry, and the Chinese he knew in the U.S.A. since he was 3 years old, have influenced his life and work. It is amazing to find that he has written as many as ten poems for Alexander Fu, son of his Chinese artist friend Fu Xu, from his birth to the present time when he is 18 years of age. Just from the generous numbers we can fathom how deep an affection he has for the child, reminding us of an old-fashioned Chinese grandfather's love of his own grandson, who is given a gift on every celebratory occasion. I met Fu Xu, his sister Fu Yun and their families when I stayed at Moss's. Lucky and enviable, they are all like the members of one big family dwelling happily in the rooms of Moss's poetry whose lease will be limitless. The writing style mirrors the writer's character, as a Chinese saying goes, so, in a word, the central theme of Moss's poetry is nothing but love. Needless to be translated, love transcends all.

Moss said that he was addicted to frivolity, which, I understand, is something similar to the so-called triviality of traditional Chinese poetry. Details of love and friendship are usually trivial or frivolous, but they are essential in poetry as well as daily life, while events are not. I remember Moss once told me that he knew some poets naked, which, I understand, has a meaning similar to a Chinese saying "to be as familiar with each other as wearing the same pants". Indeed, some of his best pieces, such as "The Legend of Self 2021", "Some Words for T.R. Hummer", "After Receiving a Letter", "I Miss Naomi Étienne" and "Another Birthday Poem, Written When Angel Was Almost a Day Older", are full of amusing and moving anecdotes about lives of poets and friends. They add to the unique flavor of Moss's poetry that dips deeply in the warmth of humanity.

Fu Hao
Recalling the Past That We Have Been in Heaven and Hell
Translated by himself

Recalling the past, we find that we have been in heaven and
      hell,
not because we did good, nor because we committed evil.

Both heaven and hell are under our feet,
one next to another as stairs
(only the number of hells is at least twice as many as that of
      heavens):

  hell
      hell
           heaven
              hell
                  hell
                      heaven
                  hell
              hell
           hell
      hell
  hell

and we keep walking down them
like children playing the game of divination:
not knowing where the last foot will land!

And we are not able, or more likely disdain
to turn back to tell the truth to our sucessors
(only oneself knows one's situation):
some will say we've gone or should have gone to heaven,
others may argue we've gone or must have gone to hell,
and then
all forget us.

INDEX OF TITLES

Also by Stanley Moss

Act V, Scene I
  Seven Stories Press
God Breaketh Not All Men's Heart's Alike: New and Selected Poems (1948-2019)
  Carcanet Press Ltd.
Almost Complete Poems
  Carcanet Press Ltd.
Almost Complete Poems
  Seven Stories Press
It's About Time
  Hopewell Press, Carcanet Press Ltd.
No Tear is Commonplace
  Carcanet Press Ltd.
God Breaketh Not All Men's Hearts Alike (2007)
  Seven Stories Press
Rejoicing
  Carcanet Press Ltd.,Anvil Press Poetry Ltd.
Songs of Imperfection
  Carcanet Press Ltd., Anvil Press Poetry Ltd.
A History of Color
  Seven Stories Press
August Follies: satyr song, a poem, and prose parables
  Privately Printed
Asleep in the Garden
  Seven Stories Press, Carcanet Press Ltd., Anvil Press Poetry Ltd.
The Intelligence of Clouds
  Harcourt Brace Jovanovich, Carcanet Press Ltd., Anvil Press Poetry Ltd.
Skull of Adam
  Horizon Press, Carcanet Press Ltd., Anvil Press Poetry Ltd.
The Wrong Angel
  Macmillan, Carcanet Press Ltd., Anvil Press Poetry Ltd.
Gedichte
  translated by Hans Magnus Enzenberger, Hanser
Selected Poems
  translated by Fu Hao, Chongquing University Press
Ya Era Hora
  translated by Valarie Mejer, Syracuse University Press

Stanley Moss was born in Woodhaven, Queens in 1925. He started writing poetry eighty-nine years ago. He enlisted in the US Navy when he was seventeen. He was educated at Trinity College and Yale University. He worked as an editor at New Directions, New American Library, *Book Week*, and *New American Review*. He taught English in Barcelona and Rome and worked at Botteghe Oscure. He taught briefly in China and Japan. In 1977, he founded Sheep Meadow Press, a nonprofit publishing company that publishes poetry and belles lettres. He is translated into German by Hans Magnus Enzenberger, into Chinese by Fu Hao, and into Spanish by Valerie Mejer. He makes his living as a private art dealer, largely in Spanish and Italian Old Masters. He lives on a farm in Clinton Corners, New York.